Zula Remembers

◆ ◆ ◆

South Arlington in Earlier Times

by
Zula Dietrich

Published by Loft Press, Inc.

P.O. Box 150, Fort Valley, VA 22652

www.loftpress.com

ISBN 1-893846-63-6

First printing

The pictures of the fire house and the old library building at 23rd and Eads Streets
on page 25 courtesy of Harold "Buddy" LeRoy.
Picture of Arlington Beach on page 25 courtesy of Robert McAtee.
Picture of 23rd and South Fern Streets on the back cover comes from
the Calvary Methodist yearbook of 1946.

Designed and typeset by AAH Graphics, Inc., Fort Valley, Virginia
www.aahgraphics.com

Foreword

ONE DAY ABOUT A YEAR AGO, LES GARRISON, MY GOOD FRIEND, neighbor, and former President of the Aurora-Highland Civic Association, asked if I would be willing to write and share with the civic association membership a few memory pieces about our neighborhood in its early days. Well, one memory led to another memory, which led to another and another until, in response to numerous suggestions from local residents, my youngest son, Mark Latsios, arranged to have them put together in a book.

I do not pretend to be a historian. I am just passing on to you some of my personal warm memories of the Aurora Hills/Virginia Highlands community during what is now a bygone era.

I want to thank my dear friends and former neighbors, Ann and Steve Hunter, for their unfailing encouragement and willingness to take on the formidable task of compiling, editing, and printing this book. Without Les's idea, Mark's generosity and persistence, and the Hunters' expertise there would be no book.

I hope you will enjoy reading these stories as much as I have enjoyed writing them.

Zula Dietrich, September 2005

Table of

Contents

THINGS TO DO

In loving memory of my parents, Sallie and Elmer Dietrich, whose brave pioneering spirit led them to settle in Aurora Hills in 1923

Memories are treasures of the heart.

JulsDietrich
2005

People

Previous page, clockwise from top left

Zula in 1934
(The Big Switch, page 17)

The Chevy II
(Miracle on 25th Street, page 25)

Zula and Nick Latsios on Wedding Day, 1944
(The Bunny Hop, page 7)

Zula and sister Winifred
(Marjorie Prythrick, page 19)

Zula and Winifred with Mrs. Prythrick in her Iris garden

Chicken Every Sunday

WHEN MY FATHER DECIDED TO BUILD A GARAGE AT OUR HOUSE, he placed it about eight feet from both the next door property line and that at the rear of our lot. He did that so that he would have a nice-sized L-shaped area on the side of the garage and at the back. Then he built a little chicken house in the far corner, fenced in the area and put an attractive large white garden gate at the front. The chicken yard was thus pretty much out of sight, but productive. We had all the eggs we could use and fried chicken quite often. Daddy would go out to the yard, pick out his victim and methodically chop off its head as I watched in horror. However, I didn't mind those fried chicken wings at all! And every year we had a brood of baby chicks that were raised to adulthood and expected to provide us with eggs and Sunday dinner.

Once my father brought home two bantam roosters with beautiful bright feathers and long, sharp spurs on their legs. They really were the Rulers of the Realm. One day when my father went into the chicken yard, one of the roosters decided to attack him. My father, in self defense, kicked toward the rooster and broke its wing. From then on that rooster had a sagging wing and a distinct limp. As time went on a prim little bantam hen joined the crowd, and then as nature would have it, along came adorable bantam chicks. The bantam population was not destined to end up on our Sunday dinner table. They were just for decoration or for giving away to any interested takers.

Young, half-grown chickens were called pullets, and they

were kept in a separate low, totally enclosed on the top and sides, wire pen until they were big enough to stand up for themselves in the regular chicken yard.

One summer's day a great thunder storm descended on the area. While that was going on a neighbor's German shepherd dog came calling, tore down the wire roof, killed a number of the pullets and dragged them back to his house to show what a great warrior he was! Everybody concerned was sorry about the incident, but all was forgiven and life went on as usual in our backyard.

Just imagine! There really was a time in this bustling neighborhood when chickens were raised in backyards, dogs could run free all over the place, and rabbits and ducks were welcome, too. But that was then and this is now. No livestock allowed!

That Old House

THE 500 BLOCK OF FRAZIER AVENUE (NOW 23RD STREET) WAS
the most populated area in Aurora Hills and Virginia Highlands
when those subdivisions were first being developed in the early
1900s. Gradually over the years, as commercial establishments
moved in, most of the houses were either destroyed or hidden
behind new fronts and additions. Amazingly, one of those houses
still stands unchanged—right smack in the middle of the north
side of that block—holding its own between (what else?) two restaurants. (Its "twin" was razed several years ago and in its place
now stands the Deluxe Diner.)

The neighborhood is fortunate to have a beautiful lady still
living here in Aurora Hills who was born in that still-standing
house. When it was the St. Elmo's Coffee Shop a few years ago, the
management was delighted to give her a guided tour of the house,
and she identified the exact room where she was born. Her family
lived there until she was about seven years old, and then moved to
a much larger home that they had built a couple of blocks away.
When the three children grew up and moved out, their parents
simply moved into a smaller home right behind the other one,
where they spent the rest of their lives. The two girls in the family
stayed in Aurora Hills and raised their own families there. One of
those daughters is the beautiful lady mentioned above.

Both she and her late husband—whose family also moved to
Virginia Highlands in the very early days—were more than very
active in all the activities at Calvary Methodist Church, where

they sang in the choir for many years. They were also very influential and totally involved in the civic and social life of the neighborhood. This lady was a bridesmaid in my sister's wedding, and her daughter and my daughter have been life-long friends.

Anyone know who she is?

The Bunny Hop

ALL SORTS OF MISGIVINGS WERE BOUNCING AROUND IN MY head about going to a dance with someone I had just met at a friend's party in my Arlington neighborhood. The boy was actually very pleasant and really rather attractive. His dancing wasn't bad either—not Fred Astaire, of course, but more than just OK. Before the night was over, he had asked me to "The Bunny Hop," his high school's spring dance. I thought it was a catchy name for a dance at Easter time and wished my sorority had come up with something as clever.

Maybe I had been a bit too hasty in accepting! I didn't know one other person from George Washington High School in Alexandria. I didn't even go to school in Virginia! Did I really want to venture into that strange place not knowing how a Little Miss Nobody from a Washington, D.C., school would be greeted? Maybe none of the boys would "cut in" and my date would be stuck with me all evening. He would be just as humiliated as I. And so I kept torturing myself like this, all the while dreaming up more and more reasons to break the date.

Mother would have none of this. I was not to break the date and that was that. She leaned heavily on a lot of things like promises, and honor and integrity. I got the point. There was no escape.

I approached the gym with caution. Well, the alien territory, as I immediately discovered, was inhabited by a happy horde of young, familiar-looking creatures called jitterbugs. We even spoke the same language, and they all wanted to meet the new girl. It was "cut-in" time at the Bunny Hop! I must have danced with most of the boys there, and every one of them told me that I looked just like one of their classmates who wasn't at the dance because she was sick. Oh, but she *was* there! She was my little guardian angel.

Toward the end of the evening, Nick,[1] one of the big men on campus, cornered my date and said, "Billie, I just want you to know that I'm going to take your girl away from you."

The handsome big man on campus cut in again. Just before I laughed merrily and danced off with my next partner, he whispered, "I want you to be a good little girl, because I am going to marry you some day."

And he did!

---

1 Nick Latsios, who is in the Washington, D.C. Boxing Hall of Fame, was a Golden Gloves boxing champion and world-ranked welter-weight professional fighter. After his military service in World War II, he went on to become a well-known restauranteur.

Come Right In

WHEN THEY CAME TO OUR COMMUNITY AFTER A MILITARY TOUR of duty in Nicaragua, the family brought with them a beautiful green and yellow full-grown parrot. I can't remember the family name, but I'll never forget the parrot—La Rita! The military being what it is, after several years, the family got new marching orders. This time it was impossible for them to take the parrot. What to do? My mother said we would take La Rita and care for her. And that is what we did. We not only took care of her we learned to love her. She was a wonderful addition to our household.

La Rita had a big cage which I had the pleasure of cleaning every day. (And parrots can be pretty messy.) She loved having her morning coffee right along with my parents, but took hers with cream and broken up bits of toast! Sunflower seeds were a staple in her diet, and we could feed them to her by hand if we were inclined to do so. With her sharp fierce looking beak, standard equipment for parrots, she took each seed gently from our fingers. Perched on a broom handle, she loved to be taken outside to watch the kids play their games, where she was the center of attention.

And La Rita could talk! She made sure you knew that her name was La Rita. Every time the phone rang, she would call, "Zula," just as she had heard my mother do so many times. A knock on the door might prompt her to call, "Mrs. Dietrich," as the neighbors often did. After the knock, she would call out and advise potential visitors to "come right in" (quoting my mother).

This proved to be a bit frustrating upon occasion when visitors were told to "come right in" when the family was away and the door was locked! A few things she brought with her from her earlier life—a Spanish phrase here and there—but her best act was when she would sway back and forth on her perch in obvious misery, cry just like a baby, and say, "I want my Mama," over and over.

La Rita loved to sit outside on the top of her cage and, spreading her wings wide, enjoy a summer's fine mist shower from the garden hose. However, one day I had her on top of the cage but forgot to turn the nozzle onto the "spray" function. When I turned the water on at the spigot, it shot from the hose with a great flourish and noise. A loud "Aw-k-k-k" pierced the air as La Rita took off like a bullet. I didn't even know she knew how to fly, but fly she did—but where? I dashed up and down the street and all around the yard calling her name. Soon one of our neighbors called to me and said that La Rita was sitting in the foliage on a trellis by her front porch. Poor La Rita was so confused. Quick as a flash, I took myself and a broom handle over there and presented it to her. She hopped on and we came home where she enjoyed an extra long spraying session that day.

And so we enjoyed La Rita for several years. But, alas, one sad day the military family came back and reclaimed her. I thought that we had earned squatters' rights and were entitled to keep her, but my mother didn't want to be difficult. So away went La Rita. Once in a while after she had moved on I would wonder if La Rita was still calling my name when the phone rang, or if she invited visitors to "come right in" at her new home.

The Most Important Day of My Life

HOW DO YOU MEASURE EXACTLY WHAT COULD BE CONSIDERED the most important day in your life? I've gone back over my memories of all the good times, the bad times, the fun times, the sad times, the successes and the failures, my marriage, my career and my social experiences, and I think that I have come up with what I can honestly call The Most Important Day of My Life: It was the day I did not die.

* * *

Everyone in the family was looking forward to our new baby. My other three children—a daughter 11 years old, a son 9 years old and a son 8 years old, and my Mother, were all waiting to hear news from the hospital that foggy, rainy first day of spring. The news finally came: We had a beautiful, perfect 9-pound boy![2]

My husband had left the hospital to get me something good to eat (probably ice cream, since he knew that was my very favorite food), when my sister-in-law, a nurse who was with me in my hospital room, realized that we had a big problem. My husband returned to the hospital just in time to see me being wheeled down the hall to the operating room.

When I heard the doctor tell him, "She's already lost so much

---

2   My youngest son, Mark Alexander Latsios.

blood I must find the reason immediately and fix it, or we will lose her," I looked up at the big lights over the operating table and said to myself, "Dear God, four kids and here I go!"

Well, the rest is history. I didn't "go". Instead, I got to raise my four children, see all their Little League games—baseball, football and basketball—watch all the dance recitals, buy the prom dresses, worry when they were out at night, and live to see all of them grow up into well-educated, successful, responsible and handsome adults.

Who can say how their lives would have turned out had I died that day? I thank the Lord that no one had to ever find out, and that I was around to have some influence on their lives. Those four little kids certainly enriched *my* life.

And, so, that's it, folks—March 21, 1958—the day more than 47 years ago that could have been the end of my story.

Old Williams

WHEN WASHINGTON AVENUE WAS THE LAST STREET IN Aurora Hills, there were still many vacant lots and straggly fields throughout the area. That's where Old Williams came into the picture. He was hired by either the county or the developers to keep those vacant lots mowed and presentable.

Old Williams lived in a small cottage on the southern side of Washington Avenue in the middle of the 300 block (now the 700 block of 26th Street, So.) He had a big mowing machine that was powered by a friendly and faithful mule. The mule was also a resident at that address. Old Williams and his mule were just a part of early Aurora Hills, and everyone was fond of them both and enjoyed watching them as they clopped-clopped around the neighbor keeping all those lots neat and appealing.

As far as I can remember, he and the mule had that side of the 700 block to themselves for a number of years. However, I have no idea when Old Williams, the mowing machine and the mule became history. But history they became and so did the unsold vacant lots!

Except that there were no curbs in Aurora Hills in those days, you might say that Old Williams already understood and cared about "Curb Appeal"!

No Kids Allowed

WE'LL CALL THEM MR. AND MRS. BROWN, AND THEY HAD NO children. They didn't like kids and they let us know it. Unfortunately for them, they lived in the middle of a block that was teeming with kids—all shapes, kinds and ages!

We kids played dodge ball and soft ball in the street, where we also held double-Dutch jump rope contests. We drew intricate hopscotch courses on the sidewalk with hunks of soft coal—but never on the Browns' side! And of course the sidewalks served as our very own and only roller skating rinks! The Browns were not amused by any of this, and we were all "afraid" of them. So, when a stray ball ended up behind the thick hedge that encircled their yard, my father was elected to retrieve it, because he wouldn't put up with their nonsense. In the spring and summer months we would have far-reaching hide-and-go-seek games. Whoever was IT at any given time did not have to worry about anyone hiding near the Browns' house. That was the only off-limits area for several blocks.

Speaking of hide-and-go-seek games—I had just been freed from seven weeks in a body cast and had graduated into a wheel chair. There was a big game underway in the next block, so I got myself rolled up there in my wheel chair with my stiff left leg extended on a support straight out in front. My mother had draped a light blanket over my legs, and away I went. It turned out that hiding under my blanket and extended left leg was the best hiding place of all—one of my friends discovered that quickly. IT never did figure it out!

Finally, the Browns moved away. No doubt they were happy to escape our innocent frolics, and we were once again free as the breeze. I *do* remember their real names and, if they are reading this right now, I hope they know that we all grew up to be acceptable adults in spite of ourselves and we hold no grudges!

The Big Switch

SHE KNEW HE WAS MY BOY FRIEND! EVERYBODY KNEW IT. HE and maybe a friend or two would ride bicycles to my house from his neighborhood about a mile away every Wednesday evening, because that was when our little rural library was open. So why did she—who just happened to be the prettiest darn 12-year old in the whole neighborhood—hop on the cross-bar of my boy friend's bicycle that particular Wednesday, and how did I end up on the green bike with someone I didn't even know? It just happened, suddenly, without planning or reason or thinking about it. Oh, well, what's three blocks on a stranger's bike?

The first thing I saw as we turned into Frazier Avenue (now 23rd Street) in front of the library was the blinding glare of headlights. Then everything went into slow motion. As I looked down at the bicycle wheel turning, turning, ever so slowly, it hit the car right between those terrifying lights. Suddenly, there I was under the car, one of its wheels resting with unquestioned authority on my right hand. Strangely, nothing hurt, but somehow I knew I was all alone and in big trouble. Quick as a flash the rescue squad came to help me, and I remember telling them, "Be very careful. My leg is broken." The stricken, horrified look in my friend's grave, yet beautiful, brown eyes as she watched them take me away on the stretcher will haunt me forever.

What a convenient place to have an accident! There was my mother working in her beloved library. Right across the street was the fire department and rescue squad. To top that off, my sister's boy friend was visiting, and he had a car. Daddy was a checkers champ and played checkers every Wednesday night at the Arizona Hotel in Washington, D.C., so he wasn't hard to find. That was the only time my father ever got up from the table and walked out in the middle of a checkers game in his entire life.

When my father saw the X-rays of my leg, he promptly fainted. Our family doctor thought that there was only one doctor in the area (in the whole United States of America actually) who might be able to reconstruct my leg, but he was out of town. So I just waited in the hospital with my traction splint and ice packs. Finally, ten days later, that marvelous, miracle-worker and his team of experts put me back together again. After six weeks in a body cast, I graduated into a wheelchair, and then came the crutches. One day to entertain myself a little, I added roller skates to the equipment. However, just as I was getting the hang of it, a highly distraught neighbor came rushing in to tell my mother that I was roller skating down the sidewalk on my crutches! So it was back to the jigsaw puzzles for me.

Things were looking up. My teachers had promoted me to the ninth grade even though I had missed a big chunk of the eighth—which, I like to think, explains why I have never been really good friends with decimals and fractions. As I got out of the car on the first day of the fall semester, I handed my father my crutches and walked into the school—not steadily or gracefully, but very proudly and thankfully.

I never knew that boy's name. I never saw him again. His green bike remained on our front porch all crippled and sad for quite a while, but no one ever came to claim it. He just rode in from nowhere, changed my life and disappeared.

Marjorie Prythrick

ALTHOUGH I NEVER KNEW HOW TO SPELL HER NAME, MARJORIE Prythrick is—at least for me—the most unforgettable character of the early Aurora Hills years. She and her husband lived in a house directly across the street from a house on Greene Avenue (now 25th St.) that my parents bought in 1923. Both houses were built in 1920 and the Prythricks were probably the first owners of theirs.

They had a big, beautiful black and white collie dog, but no children. Mrs. Prythrick—as I, of course, always addressed her— paid a lot of attention to my older sister and me. It was a joy to be around her.

She had beautiful very dark brown hair—or was it black?— that was always worn in the latest carefree style. A talented artist, she was flamboyant in her dress and in everything she did. Margie Prythrick was avant garde to the nth degree.

Deep beds of tall bright purple iris ran down both sides of her property, and a small child could disappear from view among them. On the edge of one of those iris beds was a rustic bent rattan garden settee, and hanging on the wall of my computer room right now is a picture, hand-tinted by Margie Prythrick, of me and my sister sitting side-by-side on that settee in that very special spot so many, many years ago!

In the very early days, the county maintained a Well Baby Clinic in a building on the corner of 23rd and S. Eads Street (which later became an Arlington County Branch Library), and it was Margie Prythrick who painted wonderful Mother Goose murals on the walls. In later years some of her paintings decorated other public buildings as they sprang up in the neighborhood.

For some reason when I was still quite young the Prythricks moved to a house at the corner of 24th and S. Hayes Street.[3] When her marriage ended and Mr. Prythrick left the area, thankfully, Margie stayed with us. Before too long she designed, had built, and moved into a lovely little red brick and brown shingled house with a matching double garage with an apartment over it on her lot immediately behind the bigger house. The neighborhood folks were so proud when her charming house won a Good Housekeeping design award shortly after it was built. Margie stayed in the neighborhood for quite a few more years, until age threatened and California beckoned. Then off she went—as exotic as ever!

That wonderful little house is still poised right in the middle of the block on S. Hayes St. between 23rd and 24th Streets. I do hope some of Margie's forward-thinking features and personal artistic touches have survived.

Marjorie Prythrick was not only a beautiful, interesting and talented lady, she was truly a pioneer in Aurora Hills.

---

3   I believe that house has since been razed.

An Angel in Disguise

SHE WAS VERY BEAUTIFUL STANDING UP THERE TALL AND GRACE-
ful in front of the pulpit at Calvary Methodist Church. It was
probably in the mid-to-late '30s that Rev. Betschler brought her
to our church for a week-long series of evangelical meetings. She
always wore lovely long silk garments with full length dolman
sleeves. I attended every service with great anticipation and hung
onto her every word. She carried me to places my young mind had
never gone before.

The words are gone from memory today, but the visual image
remains: At the end of each sermon she would raise her arms up
high and wide, inviting us to the altar for prayer and consultation.
As she did that, those sleeves unfurled and looked just like the
wings of an angel. Down through the years I've often thought
about Coretta Mason who, right before my young and wondering
eyes, dramatically transformed herself into a heavenly angel.

Two Birds with One Stone

WHEN I WAS GROWING UP, OUR NEXT DOOR NEIGHBOR HAD beautiful hardwood floors in her lovely entry hall and in the living and dining rooms. She was proud of them and took very good care of them.

She was a devout Jehovah's Witness and had weekly Bible study meetings in her home for many, many years. You can be sure that her front room was always ready for company. About twice each year she would take it upon herself to clean and rewax those beautiful floors. She didn't have all of the advanced cleaning products available today, so this was truly a laborious and onerous task—a real labor of love.

Finally the floor was ready for the wax and word would get out to the kids on the block. And we knew exactly what to do— find a pair of slightly over-the-hill heavy socks and a piece of an old blanket or a big old towel usually used to dry off the dog after her bath. Then we would present ourselves at the door, ready for the fun to begin.

We would skate and slide all over those floors—back and forth, up and down. The smaller kids would sit down in the middle of a big towel or piece of blanket and a couple stronger kids would hold the ends together and swing this package around and around. So, in effect, the floor was polished to a high shine by the seat of our pants and the shuffle of little soft feet. It was almost as good as an afternoon at the amusement park, and a lot cheaper!

We killed two birds with one stone—Mrs. Moore had beautifully waxed floors and we kids had a wonderful time waxing them.

Che Miracle on Twenty-fifth Street

THINGS WERE NOT GOING VERY WELL. IN FACT, THINGS WERE going straight downhill—fast.

My husband never worked for anyone else. He always had his own business and, through the years, had gone into one and out of another. So business "ups" and "downs" were just a part of our life. Lost or sold or traded away in the shuffle were three airports and several other ventures, and now our beautiful restaurant was going to die. But this time it was different—so heartbreakingly final and personal. And we had no control over what was happening.

Back in the late '50s or early '60s my husband opened the first up-scale steak house on King Street in Alexandria. He painted the building's brick facade black; the shutters were grey. All the city managers were, to put it mildly, horrified. But, try as they might, they could find no code violations. So the building remained black as ink and soon it was considered very artistic and "trendy".

Just as the restaurant was about to celebrate its third birthday, and maybe start paying for itself, the City of Alexandria put an urban renewal program into full swing. They were creating what is now called Old Town. To carry out the plans, many buildings that were not designated "historically significant," at the lower end of King Street, had to be torn down.

Sadly, the steak house building had to go. In no time at all,

25

along came that big, cruel steel ball, and down went the building—and along with it went everything we had put in it. The owner of the building was paid a handsome sum, but we were down to nothing but a lot of debt, the house we lived in, and one car. I no longer had my very own Cadillac. My husband had to declare bankruptcy—a new and humiliating experience.

Christmas was upon us. Our past Christmases had always been—even in some of our "down" times—rather lavish. This Christmas would have to be different. Somehow we managed to get a nice Christmas together for the children, but I certainly didn't expect to have my usual flood of lovely gifts. When I opened my husband's gift and found a string of cultured pearls, I was very surprised and wondered how it could be.

After everyone had opened their gifts and things settled down, my husband asked my oldest son to go with him on an errand. Soon he came back in and asked me to come outside for a minute. He wanted to show me something. There at the curb stood a little beige Chevy II. He handed me a set of keys and said, "Merry Christmas."

I just lost it, right then and there. I broke down into uncontrollable sobs. So, OK, it wasn't a Cadillac Coupe deVille. So it was a used Hertz car taken out of service and sold off the lot. But, to me, it was the most beautiful car I had ever seen. It was a Gift from Heaven. It was truly my Miracle on Twenty-Fifth Street.

Places

Previous page, clockwise from top left

Terre Latsios and Jeff Golden at one of the
Friday night dances at Calvary Church
(More than a Church, page 29)

Nick Latsios at the Minute Grill with his boxing
pictures on the wall
(The Minute Grill, page 59)

Arlington Beach
(Arlington Beach, page 55)

Old Fire Station at 23rd and Eads Streets
(The Hub, page 77)

More Than a Church

(Then and Now)

ONCE UPON A LONG TIME AGO, I WAS IN THE CRADLE ROLL SUNday School class in the little white wooden chapel at Calvary Protestant Methodist Church. Recently, Calvary United Methodist Church honored those of us, like me, who have been members of the church for 40 years or more. That spans a lifetime for both the church and for me—lifetimes of changes and memories.

Calvary Church has stood at the corner of 23rd and S. Grant Streets for all those years, doing much more than just "preaching the gospel." It was the first church in our neighborhood, and has from the very beginning established itself as a strong leader and supporter of all community activities.

Rev. Thomas Betschler, his lovely wife, Ruth, and infant daughter, Mary, came to Calvary in the Spring of 1934. They stayed there until his death in 1947. That was a rather long tenure for one preacher at one church, but we didn't ever want to let him leave.

I love to remember that Mrs. Betschler never called her husband by his given name. To her he was always "Hub." And what a joy to see Rev. Betschler in the pulpit on Sunday mornings wearing his grey-striped morning trousers and black swallow-tailed coat. Now that's preaching "hell fire and brimstone" with class!

When the Betschlers first arrived at Calvary, I was still on crutches after my bicycle accident. A couple of weeks later Mrs. Betschler—still trying to get to know all the new faces—was chatting with a group of us and asked, "What happened to that little girl on crutches?" "That's me," I said, raising my hand and taking on my new "crutcher-less" identity at the same time.

A few years after Rev. Betschler passed away, the church installed our wonderful carillon bells in his memory. The bells were programmed to ring at noon and 6:00 p.m. every weekday, and generations of children since then have been told, "Come home when you hear the bells." Rev. Betschler would have liked that!

In the mid-'50s a small group of mothers on my street got together and formed a little do-it-yourself morning kindergarten for the children. We took turns being the teacher, but met in the basement of the same house every day. Somehow the church heard about it and offered us space and equipment in its pre-school department—little chairs and all. Being in that environment made it seem more authentic and much more comfortable.

Under the leadership of Don Henretty, the early Christian Endeavor program grew into a vital Methodist Youth Fellowship that coaxed our young teens into the church every Sunday evening to enjoy a good time in a wholesome environment. In the late '50s and early '60s, the church even sanctioned dancing on the premises. Young folks from the entire community, regardless of church affiliation, came out in force to those popular Friday night dances in Harris Hall.

The church opened its doors to the Boy Scouts of America and the Cub Scouts, and they have met and conducted their activities there for many years. The Calvary Methodist-sponsored

Little League baseball team named the Tigers (coached by my husband and, later, my son-in-law) was a huge success. Rev. Bernard Via (pastor from 1964 to 1972)—whose son, Bernard, played on the team along with my son Mark—was an avid baseball fan and came to all of the games as well as many of the practices—and not just because his son played on the team. He truly loved being a part of the program.[4]

How we all looked forward to the annual church bazaar! There was a sea of tables all around Harris Hall, laden with everything you could think of to buy—all kinds of crafts and beautiful things. You could take care of your whole Christmas gift list right there. You could be with your friends, and you could eat until you couldn't hold another cookie or piece of homemade candy. Later, you could come back and enjoy a dinner prepared and served by the diligent and devoted members of the Women's Society.

At Halloween, in the mid-to-late '50s, the older grade school children donned their costumes to go "trick or treating" for less-fortunate children. The church provided each child with a small milk carton with the UNICEF emblem on it. So, instead of candy and other treats, they collected spare change for UNICEF. Afterwards, everyone returned to a well-decorated Harris Hall where they proudly emptied their cartons of coins into a big container, and a Halloween party with all the sweet trimmings got under way.

Rev. Glen Evans (pastor from 1993 to 2000) spearheaded the establishment of the extraordinarily successful Calvary Pre-School. The school is designed for little people from two years old

---

4   It is memorable to note that a neighbor, Mr. Ken Folsom, was considered the coach emeritus of the Calvary Tigers.

to kindergarten age. They attend school from 10:00 a.m. to 2:00 p.m., five days a week. So popular is the program that the enrollment waiting list is long (60 or more) at any given time. Beth Posey is the wonderfully talented and well-qualified Director.

And Calvary United Methodist Church is still doing it! At the last presidential election, Calvary opened Harris Hall and did a brisk business serving delicious sandwiches and beverages free to anyone who could produce an "I Voted" sticker. What a fine and generous way for a church to support our democratic process!

When I read the weekly bulletin, I think I wouldn't mind being a kid again, to take part in the innovative and interesting activities planned every week. Christian, moral and social principles are being learned by those young people—whether they realize it or not—through varied activities that are not only fun, but also prepare them for a rich and happy time throughout their lives.

If you should wonder why I am always proud to tell someone that I belong to Calvary United Methodist Church at 23rd and S. Grant Streets, please read this little article again.

The Little Station

IT WAS CUTEST THING IN THE WHOLE NEIGHBORHOOD. NEVER
mind that the streetcar line was long gone. Never mind that there
were schools, churches, grocery and hardware stores and all sorts
of other establishments to make our life easier. Why did "they"
take away the wonderful little trolley car station at 26th and S.
Eads Streets?

That station was an artistic miniature replica of a railway station anywhere in America. It was red brick, and it had benches
just like the big stations. There was a ticket window and it even
had rest rooms (a real luxury in those days)! There was a sidewalk
all the way around and, in its heyday, nobody cared if the kids
tried out their roller skates there. It was even used by the founding fathers of Calvary Methodist Church for Sunday morning services. And long after the trolley car line was replaced by busses on
Route 1, the little station stood there proud and quaint reminding all of us of earlier days. We cherished it.

The station was a very important historical part of our community. Its picture appears on an early real estate presentation
designed to sell building lots here in Aurora Hills[5].

I don't remember when our station went away. It just wasn't
there any more one day. I can only assume that it fell victim to the

5   The advertisement (dated October 1922) announces that the lots cost 12 to 15 cents per
square foot. A deposit of $25.00 was required, with monthly payments of $12.00. There
was a discount for cash and an extra discount if you started building your home within 60
days of your lot purchase. As the song goes, "Those Were the Days."

widening of Route 1 and S. Eads Street as they passed through the community. Whenever it went, it shouldn't have gone, and I doubt that I am the only one of the Old Brigade who regrets someone's decision about what to do with our little trolley car station. It was a true gem!

The Gray Ghost of Jubal Early

BEFORE WORLD WAR II, WASHINGTON, D.C., WAS JUST A slightly sleepy big "small town" with a subtle aura of power and prestige. It was beautiful and peaceful, with everything you could ask for, from housing to schools to entertainment to fine dining— and lots of happy, friendly dyed in the wool "natives."

Downtown meant F Street, NW, and the surrounding area, where all kinds of shops, theaters and restaurants lined both sides of the streets from 15th to 7th Streets, NW. You would be sure to run into a couple of friends on any given trip to Woodies[6], the Fox (later renamed the Capitol) Theater, historic Reeves, the Neptune Room[7] or even Murphy's[8] music counter, where a gal would play all the latest tunes on the piano. You could even spin records on their turntable; likewise at Jordan's Music Store around the corner on G Street—no obligation to buy! There were at least six movie houses in that downtown area, two of which offered, along with the movie, live stage shows featuring big-name entertainers—like Red Skelton, Judy Garland and Mickey Rooney.

But a war was raging in Europe, and sabers were rattling all around the world. Things were changing with frightening speed in our town as thousands of people from all over the country

6   Woodward and Lothrop, an upper-end department store
7   A popular restaurant/bar.
8   Murphy's was a large "five and ten cent" store.

flocked to the nation's capital, because our government needed all the help it could get. We soon found ourselves fighting a war on two fronts, and D.C. was literally bursting at the seams. Where were all of these people going to live? What was happening to our home town? It obviously would never, ever be the same.

South Arlington to the rescue! Suddenly, out of nowhere, a low-rent, war-time housing project rose from the ground, right here in our own back yard. Named for a Confederate general, the Jubal Early Homes complex was constructed in the low-lying area from 22nd Street, So. to 18th Street, So. between S. Eads and S. Fern Streets.[9] It consisted of row upon row of nondescript concrete two-story structures containing four apartments each. Each building was firmly anchored on a big concrete slab.[10] The Jubal Early Homes were razed sometime in the mid '50s, but 'tis said that the general's gray ghost roamed silently among those acres of naked concrete slabs for a few more years.

Bleak or not, that housing project served its purpose and the country very well, and our community was proud to be its host.

By the way, has anyone seen a displaced gray ghost lately?

---

9   This is where Crystal House One and Crystal House Two were later built.

10 An identical complex called The Shirley Homes was built at the same time on S. Lang Street on that whole tract of land now occupied by the Gunston Recreation Center, a live-performance theater, and Gunston Junior High School.

Potomac Yards

WHENEVER I DRIVE FROM MY HOME IN AURORA HILLS DOWN Route 1 toward Alexandria, it isn't long before I begin to feel as if I am entering a foreign country. Instead of acres of freight trains getting themselves organized into trains to the south and to the north, there is the Potomac Yards strip mall with its acres of parked cars. And what are they going to build on top of all that red Virginia clay that is spread around over more acres to the north—more apartments and retail stores? The little businesses that helped us with our ailing cars, empty gas tanks, bald auto tires and other such mundane problems are gone, and in their place are fancy and expensive condos reaching to the skies.

I like to remember the original Potomac Yards. It was like a giant central post office. But instead of dealing with letters and packages going everywhere, it disbursed big freight cars, which had to be joined together into long freight trains destined for cities all up and down the East Coast. How they did it always intrigued me. There were no computers or other wireless fancy contraptions in those days to ease the task. They used a reverberating loud speaker system. When I was a child, on a still summer's night as I lay in my bed on our sleeping porch with those big windows open, I could sometimes hear the men calling over that loud speaker as they "made up" the trains.

To cross the Yards from Route 1, the many employees used a set of iron steps with railings that led to a raised walkway above and across the many lanes of railway tracks. The Potomac Yards

Bridge still carries Route 1 auto traffic across that tract of land, but, alas, the wonderful ice house on the east side of the bridge is no more.

That ice house had a large open deck where the refrigerated cars were loaded with huge chunks of ice for their trip to wherever they were going with whatever they were carrying. But the ice house remains in our family's memory because that's where we went for the ice to make hand-churned ice cream for special occasions, or just because we were in the mood. The strong man on duty would spear a huge square of ice, drag it out on the side deck, and then cut off whatever amount we needed. You could also buy big brown paper bags of crushed ice. Just going down to the ice house was always an adventure.

Today, more goods are transported all over the United States by big trucks and tankers on the highways than by freight trains on the railway tracks. And it isn't always pleasant to play "dodge me if you can" with those huge vehicles out there on the interstates, especially if you are driving a little compact car that shudders in their wake.

Into the Woods

IN THE '20S AND '30S, WHEN AURORA HILLS WAS VERY YOUNG, just about everything in a large area south of the present day 26th Street, So. and S. Glebe Road, and west between S. Grant Street and Oakcrest Drive, was known as "The Woods."

The neighborhood children hiked all through those dense woods and played "war" in Ft. Scott. Swinging across the trench on grapevines ropes, they searched for Indian arrowheads, carved their initials on the trees, and encountered rabbits, squirrels and other assorted animals, as well as all kinds of birds. Prized trophies included turtles, lizards, and wildflowers . . . and sometimes even poison ivy!

Every once in a while some brave parent would take a few kids into the woods for a weenie roast. We fashioned our own spits from carefully selected small branches we found on the ground. Naturally, a few hot dogs were charred along the way, and those fluffy marshmallows seemed to have a very special knack for plopping themselves into the fire. But that was just part of the fun. We sang our favorite songs at the top of our lungs, and whooped and hollered as we circled the fire performing our version of the Indian War Dance. Other times we might just go there to gather bright fall branches and leaves. Whatever the reason, going to the woods was always a treat.

Now when I drive down Ft. Scott Drive, flashes of those days pass through my mind, and I wonder if the children in today's world of TVs, computers and cell phones are as busy and happy as my friends and I were when we just went "into the woods."

Hell's Bottom

BACK WHEN MY FATHER WAS STILL DRIVING HIS MODEL T FORD, Arlington Ridge Road did not dead-end, but continued straight across the area where the "mixing bowl" would later be built, past the low red brick wall in front of Arlington Cemetery. I don't know where it ended up. Nor did Columbia Pike end at the Pentagon South Parking Lot. It went straight east and ended at Route 1. If you can draw a straight line, you will conclude that the two should cross each other somewhere along the line. And they did.

The two roads intersected at a place affectionately called Hell's Bottom! There was a lively little clutch of housing and life-sustaining establishments stretching several blocks east and west on both sides of Columbia Pike—remnants of Freedmen's Village, a housing development built after the Civil War for freed slaves.

Alas, there are no remnants of Hell's Bottom left. All that residential area, with its rich history, was replaced by the sterile outlines of the Navy Annex, the Pentagon and Shirley Highway.

Man the Boats

IT IS SO SERENE AND HARMLESS LOOKING NOW. IT HAS NOT always been so. Once upon a time not too many years ago our little Four Mile Run frequently overflowed its banks with a vengeance. Eventually, the repetitive flooding destroyed a couple blocks of very nice homes on the southern side of S. Glebe Road between Mt. Vernon Avenue and Route 1. A whole block of business establishments in Arlandria (including a pony ride for the kids) went up in flames following one of those wide-spread floods. Finally, and thankfully, the flood control plant was built and the little stream has become a friendly neighbor. At the moment, there are plans on the drawing board for a beautification project for Four-Mile Run as it wends its way through the county.

Four-Mile Run, in flood, has carried cars from an upstream automobile dealer's lot all the way downstream to Walter Reed Drive, destroying the bridge at Walter Reed Drive and Four-Mile Run Road in the process. It moved a friend's car around in the parking lot of the Arlandria Warner Towers (now The Portals), and re-parked it for her. Next day, she came to my desk with her insurance papers in hand and told me about it. She was in a state of shock and said, "I don't understand how that happened. I had the brakes on!" That was really very funny, but it was no time to laugh! Hayman's, a popular ladies clothing shop, finally gave up after a number of floods in Arlandria, as did a little department store, a great ten-cent store, an up-scale children's clothing store, a shoe store and a full-service hardware store. After one of

Hayman's floods I bought (for $50.00) a luxurious white wool winter coat with an ermine collar. (I still have the collar.) Only one tell-tale sign revealed how high the water had gotten in the store—a very faint water line all the way around just under the arms on the white satin lining.

But all of that is forgotten, and we are looking forward to our Four-Mile Run becoming a thing of beauty and a joy forever.

Carhops and Root Beer Floats

BEFORE MCDONALDS, BEFORE HOWARD JOHNSON'S, WENDY'S, Roy Rogers, Big Boy or Jack-in-the-Box, there was Hot Shoppes. J. W. Marriott opened the first Hot Shoppe in Washington, D.C., in 1927. It was a nine-stool root beer stand. By the mid-thirties there were Hot Shoppes all around the metropolitan area. By that time they had become a lot more than root beer stands. You could get everything at the Hot Shoppes, from breakfast at any time of the day or night, to hamburgers, hot dogs, various sandwiches, bar-b-que beef, hot tamales, and other light meals. Even so, their original concept, the famous A&W Root Beer float, never went out of style or favor.

We had a number of Hot Shoppes right here in our own back yard: At the southern end of the Twin Bridges (14th Street Bridge), on the Rosslyn side of the Key Bridge, at Columbia Pike and Walter Reed Drive, and in Shirlington. Still another near-by location was at the northern end of N. Washington St., in Alexandria, as that thoroughfare turns into the George Washington Parkway on its way to D.C.

Since I went to Eastern High School in D.C., after our frat or sorority dances, my "gang" would go often to a Hot Shoppe out on Bladensburg Road. There my usual fare would be a pecan waffle and a vanilla milk shake or a root beer float. I really don't believe that there has ever been a better pecan waffle produced anywhere!

Along with all of the other wondrous memories of the Hot Shoppes, remember that you could get anything on the menu served to you in your car if that was your pleasure. A carhop took your order, and brought it to you on a tray that hooked to the door of the car at the open window! It was a lot of fun to have a car full of teenagers passing the food around and spilling it all over each other in the process. During the Vietnam War, I met a serviceman at the Pentagon who told me that for several years, as a young adult, he came up here from North Carolina to carhop all summer at the Hot Shoppes. And he had some good stories to tell about that.

Marriott Hot Shoppe, Inc., sold off all the local Hot Shoppes—one by one—closing the last one on a very sad day in 1989. Nothing following in their wake has ever replaced them for those of us who remember pecan waffles and A&W Root Beer floats, especially when one of those root beer floats was spilled on that pretty white silk evening coat that you had borrowed from your sister!

But there is a happy ending to this story. It is my understanding that the Marriott Corporation plans to convert Allie's Family Restaurant (formerly the Rosslyn Hot Shoppe) into a commemorative Hot Shoppe. It will be an exact replica of its former self, with the classic running boy logo, colors, menus, and everything. A Fall 2005 opening is anticipated.

Gone, But Not forgotten

THE BUILDING BOOM WAS IN FULL SWING IN THE CLAY PITS. A couple of north and south streets now pushed through that whole tract of land. There were also 15th Street, and two Crystal Houses at S. Eads and 18th Streets, just to mention some notable landmark changes. But I want to tell you a story about another landmark.

In about 1961, two enterprising young men got a 99-year lease on all the land between S. Eads and S. Fern on the east and west, and 15th to 18th Streets on the north and south. Anyone who has moved into the Aurora-Highlands area within the last forty years probably has no idea what those young men did, because there isn't a trace of it left. They built a sports complex of great magnitude, and they called it Pentagon City. There were two adjoining twin 40-lane bowling alleys (that's right—80 lanes!) in an *L*-shaped configuration.[11] You could walk from the entrance, at 15th and Eads Streets, all the way through to the top of the "L," at 18th and Fern Streets, without going outside. Each bowling alley had its own restaurant and snack bar, plus lounging

---

11 At the bowling alleys there was always one red pin in each frame. If that pin came up as the lead pin and the bowler scored a strike, he received a coupon for a free pizza. One evening my two older sons, who had just stepped into their teens, were there with a couple of friends watching an expert bowler play. He told the boys that if the red pin came up and he got a strike he would give them the coupon. The red pin came up; he got the strike; and, my boys got their very first taste of pizza!

areas. There were pinball machines and other electronic games in the corridors along the way, not to mention a ballroom, a billiard room, and a Pro Shop.

At the top of the "L" on 18th Street, there was an outdoor ice skating rink (the largest outdoor rink in the Metropolitan area), with a warm-up room and an ice-skate rental facility. Various hockey teams ("pick-up" and otherwise) played Saturday morning games there. Residents on the north side of the Crystal House could enjoy what was going on from their living rooms. Young teenagers would just hang on the fence and root for their favorite side. Under the lights at night, the skaters and the Crystal House residents often waved and called to each other. On the grounds but in a separate building, there was a travel agency.

Unfortunately, the owners were forced into bankruptcy and Pentagon City was closed and razed in about 1967. When that awesome complex was being dismantled all sorts of sports equipment, furnishings, and so forth were simply given away to anyone who wanted to carry or haul it away. It was really very sad.

Crystal Towers rose from the ruins, and under construction right now—where those two entrepreneurs had hoped to build a sportsmen's lodge and a miniature golf course to further enhance their sports complex—is an extremely dense arrangement of townhouses and condos snuggling as close as it can legally get to Crystal Towers.

A trade-off is a trade-off—some good, some bad! Take your pick!

Abingdon Estate

WE ALWAYS CALLED IT THE NELLIE CUSTIS HOME WHEN, IN fact, it is known historically as the Abingdon Estate and Nellie Custis really didn't live there all that long. When George Washington's stepson, John Parke Custis, and Eleanor Calvert (of the Maryland Calverts) were first married the couple lived at Mt. Vernon. After a couple of years George Washington bought the Abingdon Estate for them and they made their home there. Sadly, John Parke Custis, still a young man, died of camp fever at York-town during the Revolutionary War. Eleanor, being a new widow with four small children, had a difficult road ahead of her. To ease her burden, George and Martha Washington took the two youngest children (George Washington's step grandchildren) and raised them as their own at Mt. Vernon. George Washington Parke Custis was only six months old and Eleanor (Nellie) Custis, two and a half years old at the time. They received the best of educations and all the advantages accorded children of distinguished and wealthy families of that day.

Abingdon Estate was situated on the west bank of the Potomac River in nearly a direct line east of my own home on 25th Street in Aurora Hills. And there it remained, sometimes occupied and other times vacant, a victim of age, neglect, and fire until, finally, all that was left were a few remnants of the foundation and a plaque telling a bit of its story.

For better or for worse, Washington National Airport (now Reagan National Airport) has managed to envelop that whole area. However, accessible from the bicycle path along the Potomac, that plaque is still holding its own and telling its little story.

When I was a child, my mother, my sister, and I sometimes walked across Route 1 and the railroad tracks (very cautiously) to visit the Nellie Custis home. I remember only that it was not occupied when we visited, and we never peeked inside. Furthermore, my child mind was impressed to know that there was a well on the grounds.

As a child, I never really understood exactly who Nellie Custis was, except that she and George Washington were related in some way. I know next to nothing about what happened at the Abingdon Estate after Nellie and her baby brother were taken to Mt. Vernon. However, I do know that right here in Aurora Hills, there lives a delightful lady who was born at the Abingdon Estate in 1912 and lived there for a number of years. She well remembers that very long walk from her house on the Potomac to Hume School up on Arlington Ridge Road where she received her early education. As this area opened to development, her parents moved the family into a home in Virginia Highlands, among the first settlers there, and were very active and respected pioneers in the neighborhood.

Nellie Custis, the little toddler of Abingdon who was raised as George Washington's adopted daughter, married George Washington's nephew, Lawrence Lewis. For their wedding gift, the General gave them a large tract of land called Woodlawn Plantation. In addition, he arranged for the architect who designed the national Capitol building to design and build a lovely home there for the couple.

We are truly living in an exciting historical area, and it is stimulating to hear about and even see so many interesting things concerning the brave Colonists and those who followed in their footsteps. It makes me wonder what the historians will have to say about us should they wish to erect statues and plaques in honor of our deeds—or misdeeds—as the case may be!

Woodlawn Plantation, just a few miles west of Mt. Vernon, has survived the rigors of the years, and is open to the public on a regular schedule. Heading south on the George Washington Parkway, drive straight through Alexandria. When you get to Mt. Vernon, veer a bit to the right at the circle but stay in the left lane. Curving just slightly to the right you will come to a stop sign. Go straight at the stop sign and you will still be on the George Washington Parkway—which is exactly where you want to be—going west. Now cruise along on the Parkway a couple more miles until you reach Route 1 (Richmond Highway). Straight ahead—or maybe just a bit left of center—you'll see the entrance to Woodlawn in all its glory. Go right in!

Note: Scheduling information can be obtained by calling the Plantation (703) 780-3264.

ḣarry's Blue Bird Bar-B-Que

WHEN I WAS A CHILD I WAS VERY MUCH AWARE OF HARRY'S Blue Bird Bar-B-Que. A roadhouse of great renown and reputed wickedness, it was nestled on old Rt. 1 just south of the 14th Street Bridge near where the railway tracks crossed the road. There was always a lot of activity going on. It seemed secretive and exciting. People went in and out at all hours of the day and night. Mysterious blue lights filtered out into the darkness. Every once in a while you could catch a few notes of music on the air.

Mother confirmed my vague suspicions by her actions. Good Southern Methodist that she was, she would urge my father to keep the car in high gear as we drove by, for fear I would catch a glimpse of those evil doings and be tainted for life.

To this day I don't know what really went on inside the place, but I doubt that it could ever have been all that shocking—or could it?

Arlington Beach

(*But Don't Go Near the Water*)

WHEN MY FATHER TRADED IN HIS BIG, BLACK BICYCLE FOR A Model T Ford, I became aware of the enticing beach and small amusement park on the southern side of the 14th Street Bridge. Once we had family transportation, my father treated us to regular jaunts into D.C. On the return journey, as Daddy steered his "Tin Lizzy" across the bridge, I used to worry about the Airplane Ride at the park. Little airplanes whirled overhead, going around and around on the ends of wires. It looked as if they would surely hit us. I longed to go to the beach and play in the water, and take an up-close look at that Airplane Ride. However, it was never to be. Mother was convinced (and rightly so!) that the water was polluted and my sister and I would contract all sorts of horrible diseases should we go near the place.

In due time, Arlington Beach and its whirli-bird airplane ride disappeared, and Hoover Field (predecessor of Reagan National Airport) came to be. A few years later, a state-of-the-art swimming pool and restaurant were built at the water's edge next to the airport. All of this proved to be a great attraction for us "natives," as well as out-of-town visitors. That became just the thing to do—go and watch those wonderful and exciting, honest-to-goodness real airplanes coming and going. Never once did I imagine that someday, one of them would drop out of the sky!

It had become a whole new world.

A Drug Store—A Penny Candy Counter

IN THE STRICTEST SENSE OF THE WORD, I GUESS MCCOY'S DRUG Store wasn't really a drug store, because it did not have a pharmacy department. However, from the late '20s until the early '40s it was all we had. We loved it, and we *called* it a drug store. My close neighbors, Mr. and Mrs. McCoy, were the hard-working owners, and they did a brisk business. Things have changed so much in the 500 block of 23rd Street, it's hard to be sure, but McCoy's was either where the Mogul Restaurant currently resides or else next door in the International Bistro building.

There was the soda fountain that also served as a light lunch counter and, of course, some classic ice cream parlor table and chairs. My own special treat was to stop there once a week or so, on my way home from school in Washington, and have a ten-cent, strawberry ice cream soda. A big attraction for the neighborhood children was the penny candy counter—with its Tootsie Rolls, lollypops, licorice sticks, bubble gum and other tempting treats for just a penny each. The store also carried a complete line of patent medicines and other products to take care of our aches and pains, cuts and bruises, scrapes and itches, runny noses, coughs and sneezes. Toiletries and cosmetics, and the inevitable newspaper and magazine rack, completed McCoy's inventory.

By the mid-'30s Mr. McCoy had sold the ice cream and patent medicine drug store and moved on up the street a few stores away and opened a little restaurant. The new owner, Mr. Croft, added a pharmacy counter at that time. A few years later Dr. Henderson took over the operation.

And that was the beginning—in not too many years our little drug store had, one step at a time, evolved into the Arlington Drug Store—a much larger state-of-the-art establishment with a very nice lunch counter and two new proprietors. Our new drug store was located at the corner or 23rd and South Fern Streets, where we now have the Stars and Stripes restaurant, and 23rd Street had by that time become quite a busy little shopping area.

But, to go back to penny candy counters for a moment—although they have pretty much disappeared in the maze of big impersonal chain drug stores, they have not been forgotten. Clinging to the nostalgic past, Timberman's Drug Store (privately owned and established in Alexandria in 1856) still has *its* penny candy counter. Most of the items now cost five or ten cents, but, for old times sake, a few penny offerings linger on.

The Minute Grill

WHEN THE UNITED STATES GOVERNMENT DECIDED SUDDENLY one day in the late '40s to cancel the GI Bill of Rights for pilot instruction, my husband (now deceased) promptly lost his three airports with their flying schools—Manassas, Leesburg, and Fredericksburg—and all those cute Piper Cubs sitting in neat little rows. And so he bought the Minute Grill to pay off his airport debts and to keep his family from starving.

The Minute Grill faced Route 1 on the western side,[12] right next to the Exxon Station at 23rd Street and behind the kabob and other restaurants facing S. Eads Street. At that time, the post office, a dry cleaner and a laundromat were the Minute Grill's backdoor neighbors.

The Minute Grill was located in a small white stucco structure with a big plate glass window occupying most of its front. It had four booths and a counter with six stools. It quickly became a gathering place where locals ate breakfast before heading into the big city to work, and where the many friendly truck drivers could stop and enjoy the comradery and a hamburger. It welcomed a constant parade of tourists and, once in a while, a whole caravan of gypsies or a bus full of school kids, who would drop in and create quite a stir. It offered good frozen custard and lots of D.C. souvenirs, and featured a big and bustling fireworks stand every Fourth

---

12 Before the Interstates, and beltways, Route 1 was the official truck route from Maine to Florida.

of July. To add to the Grill's unique character, it was decorated plentifully with pictures of the owner in his Golden Gloves and professional boxing days—a good conversation piece if nothing else!

A local clique of young men kept the Minute Grill humming, gathering there in between their various business duties, telling stories and catching up on current gossip and what was happening in the world. If you wanted to see a particular friend, you could usually find him at the Minute Grill at one time or another.

The hours at the Grill were long and hard. For a while it was open 24/7, with young "moonlighting" servicemen pulling the midnight-to-dawn shift. Unfortunately, it seemed that they were stealing more than they were putting in the cash register, and that source of help was no longer attractive. So most of the time my husband, plus one other hard worker, kept the Minute Grill going from breakfast to 10:00 or 11:00 p.m.

As the fabulous '50s were drawing to a close, my husband decided to do something else with his life. He sold the Minute Grill to a local enterprisng young man. It was still the Minute Grill, but it wasn't the same without that charismatic Golden Greek owner and all those colorful characters who had frequented it in its heyday. The grill changed hands a couple more times, and in 1980 it became just another casualty of the reconfiguration of Route 1 and the building of the overpass to the airport.

That little Minute Grill will always hold a very special place in my family's heart.

Luna Park

ACCORDING TO AN ARTICLE IN THE WASHINGTON POST SUNDAY
magazine a few years ago, Luna Park was built in 1906. Today it
has been replaced by the "lovely" Arlington sewage treatment
plant on S. Eads Street just north of South Glebe Road. Luna Park
reportedly was quite an elaborate complex, with rides, a ballroom,
picnic grounds, very stylish exhibition buildings, and a circus
arena. According to the *Post,* some elephants that had been
imported from Coney Island for a show managed to create quite a
stir when they escaped! Luna Park lasted only a few years and was
razed in 1915—even before *my* time on earth.

For me, Luna Park was just the name of a once-upon-a-time
amusement park and a clutch of houses on the top of the hill
where a couple of my school friends lived. On one occasion I
arrived at a friend's house in Luna Park on pig-slaughtering day.
While the grown-ups were busy slaughtering the pig and making
sausage, the kids were playing a game of kick ball with the pig's
inflated bladder. (Well, after all, remember there were no computers at that time.)

The hill from those houses down to S. Eads Street was very
steep, and at the bottom was a man-made shallow pond, appar-
ently the remains of a Luna Park water-slide ride of some sort. The
pond gradually evolved into a great tadpole habitat, and the
neighborhood kids loved catching those wiggly things and hop-
ing they would, indeed, turn into frogs.

After the pond disappeared, all that was left was the steep

hill. When the county added an incinerator to the scenery, Sandy Cliff (as the kids called the hill) was somehow spared, and was still serving as a popular "dirt slide ride" for the neighborhood kids in the mid '50s. My two older boys wore the seat out of a number of pairs of jeans on that hill! The only thing that saved the next generation of jeans was the expansion of the incinerator into a full-blown state-of-the-art sewage treatment plant. Sandy Cliff was sacrificed, and in its place was built an unusual-looking sprawling edifice. Just for good measure, a less-than-beautiful body shop was added to the scenery mix.

Alas and alack!

The Club House and Hobos

ONCE UPON A TIME—IN THE LATE '20S AND EARLY '30S WHEN I was young and even up into the '50s when my children were young—there was a very densely wooded hill between S. Eads Street and Jefferson Davis Highway roughly from 24th Street to 26th Street. Not only was it beautiful but it hid Route 1 traffic and dulled the noise of the trains that rolled north and south right near the highway. (The tracks were moved toward the river in the late '60s, to make room for Crystal City.)

My little playmates and I had a private open-air "club house" on the very edge of those woods where 25th Street dead-ends at S. Eads Street. There we would build small fires in our crude, hand-made stone fireplace and bake mud-coated potatoes in the hot coals. We called it a feast. There were big stones and logs to sit on, and we pretended we were cowboys camping out on the range, or played tree tag and other games we made up as we went along. Since my family lived in the 500 block of 25th Street, my mother could—and did—always check on how things were going down in the club house on any given Saturday morning.

Because the train tracks were just across Route 1, the many hobos "riding the rails" in those days found our thick woods to be just the place to seek rest and refuge before continuing their train-hopping journey. Therefore, in addition to providing the pota-toes, my mother issued stern warnings regarding hobos, and explicit instructions on what to do in the event of a hobo sighting. I passed on all of that wisdom to my own children who also have fond memories of their escapades in those woods.

Best of all, there were two billboards perched on a clearing at the eastern edge of the hill facing Route 1, just a bit south of today's CVS pharmacy. It was fascinating to watch the men wielding very long-handled brushes as they created those wonderful advertisements. It was as if they were pasting huge bright jigsaw puzzles on the walls of a giant's house—not an easy task. Frankly, I missed those colorful billboards when they, the thick woods, and most of the hill were removed only to be replaced by, of all things, a sterile overpass to the airport in the exact spot where our little club house had been.

Maybe billboards will make a comeback some day, but our hill and those beautiful woods are gone forever!

Restaurant Row

IN THE '20S AND EARLY '30S, THE BEGINNING OF OUR NEIGH-
borhood, there was precious little established in Aurora Hills and
Virginia Highlands to conveniently support life except indoor
plumbing, electricity, your own vegetable garden and chicken
yard, a brave pioneer spirit and our trolley line to D.C. and Alexandria.

However, we did not go without! We were on the route for
Toby the iceman, and a variety of hucksters carrying seasonal
fruits and vegetables. Thompson's Dairy delivered milk every day.
There was an egg man, too, as well as a meat truck, where the
butcher cut your meat to order right there on a big wooden table
in the back of the truck. The Jewel Tea Company came calling, as
did the Fuller Brush man, and a little old lady named Mrs.
Ganaway with her big shopping bag taking and delivering orders
for all sorts of cooking and personal necessities, such as vanilla fla-
voring, spices, and soaps. Door-to-door salesman was the name of
the game. If you ran out of sugar or flour in the middle of making
a cake, you went to a neighbor and "borrowed" it. Everyone
always "owed" someone a cup of this or a cup of that—nobody
ever lost track either.

The 500 block of 23rd Street was all residential—just like
the other streets and avenues in the subdivision. However, as time
went on and more and more "settlers" came into the neighborhood, one by one, the houses in that block were converted into
small businesses—a couple of grocery stores, a drug store, a barber

shop, a beauty shop, a fix-it shop, and a bicycle repair shop. There were a variety store, a hardware store, and a dry cleaners. We even had a little restaurant tucked in there somewhere. Until we got own post office (on Eads St. behind the 7-11), a corner of the dry cleaning establishment served that purpose. And that was the start of our little downtown, which by the mid-'40s boasted a TV shop, a much larger drug store, a nice music store, real estate offices, and a gift shop, to mention a few. We were no longer "pioneers" but a comfortably happy and ongoing community.

Then along came Crystal City in the late '60s, and it just grew and grew and grew into full bloom, and conquered the whole eastern side of Jefferson Davis Highway. And where were all those people who worked in those big buildings supposed to spend their lunch and happy hours?

So here we go again—one by one—the shops were reincarnated—Hello Restaurant Row!

The Creek

On the October 1922 real estate developer's plat of Aurora Hills, it is called a Reservation, and wends its way diagonally through the neighborhood from the 800 block of 23rd Street (then Frazier Avenue) to the 500 block of Pierce Place (which I think is now probably S. Glebe Road). But to us early settlers it was the Creek—a shallow open little trickling stream bubbling along. It found its way under the cross streets that it encountered via big pipe tunnels. I never explored its wanderings from beginning to end, but the part of the Creek that I was aware of ran diagonally from the southeast corner of 23rd Street and S. Ives to the southeast corner of 26th Street and S. Grant.

In the old days, I had a friend who lived in the 800 block of 25th Street. When I left her house to return home, she would always say, "I'll walk you to the Creek." (which was in the 700 block). Likewise, when she visited me in the 500 block it was my turn to walk her to the Creek. It was also a good meeting place to embark on various joint adventures.

Although it seemed like a fun thing to do, my parents always warned me not to crawl through the tunnel. And, when my children were growing up here, I also let them know that crawling through the tunnel was unsafe and off limits. As for me—I never did crawl through that attractive tunnel! Boys being boys, I'm not sure whether my own sons did or did not.

Where did our little creek go? It must be somewhere down there underground—flowing along its merry way, even though we can no longer see it. Do basements sometimes flood mysteriously, or do floors crack and sag for no apparent reason? Have you ever heard its little trickling voice in the dead of night?

What do you do with a creek when you want it to not be a creek any more? If hearts and livers can be transplanted from one body to another, and men can walk on the moon, a little creek can be made to disappear. Wouldn't it be nice, though, to think that it is could still be trickling along in some lovely new place?

From Soup to Nuts

ONE OF OUR FIRST GROCERY STORES WAS A LITTLE DGS[13] ON THE southeast corner at 23rd and Hayes Streets, So. The owners were Mr. and Mrs. Taisoff, who had a beautiful young daughter named Miriam. The store was on the first floor of a reconfigured residential edifice, so that the entrance to the store was on 23rd Street while the entrance to the second-floor apartment where the Taishoffs lived was on S. Hayes Street. After a number of years, the Taishoffs—who were obviously forward-thinking people— sold the store to the Brill family, built a nice brick commercial building in the 500 block of 23rd Street, and opened up a hardware store there. Then the Taishoffs lived in a very attractive apartment on the second floor of their new building.

That friendly hardware store was a wonderful addition to our small but ever growing 23rd Street "downtown." Now we could get all of our gardening needs, home repair supplies, paint, and so on, quickly and easily instead of traveling to Alexandria or Clarendon every time we needed some little gadget or fixture. Of course, the store prospered and the Taishoffs stayed there for quite a few years. However, in due time, they sold the business to another enterprising and affable husband and wife team —the Burkas.

Community Hardware Store was an important part of our locality for a long time. It was so pleasant having such nice neigh-

13 District Grocery Store.

bors to help you find what you needed, and to enjoy a little chat and a laugh or two along the way. Sadly, Ellis Burka passed away just about the time that Crystal City was going strong and 23rd Street was being rapidly transformed from our own little downtown into "restaurant row." Two of his sons kept the store open until it was no longer feasible to do so. The restaurants had won the battle!

That building is still there; the Thai Restaurant and the Subway sandwich shop, among others, are tucked into the front. Between those two restaurants, there is a small walkway leading to a door—that could mean that there is still an occupied apartment on the second floor!

As of now, if you need a hatchet or a power hedge cutter, or whatever, it's out on the road to a Home Depot or some other large, impersonal establishment—unless, of course, you want to take a chance on misplacing your car in a parking garage in Crystal Underground where once—several years ago—I stumbled upon a small limited-edition hardware store tucked away in a corner. Even at that I probably could never find it again, try as I might. By the way, where did I park the car?

Arlington Farms

ARLINGTON FARMS WAS BUILT ON LAND THAT FOR MANY YEARS was the Department of Agricultural Experimental Farm, and although there was not a cow or a corn field to be seen, Arlington Farms it was. Actually I never knew too much about the place. It was there when I came back to Aurora Hills after living for about three years in Washington, D.C. Looking for it today, there are no signs that it ever existed.

Unique in the area, Arlington Farms was a huge, self-suffi-cient residential complex for the many, many young women who came to the area to work for the government and help in the war effort. It was located just west of the Pentagon near Ft. Myer, the Naval Annex and Arlington Cemetery

Ten clusters of buildings around a well-maintained plaza similar to a campus quad could house 8,000 girls at a time. To qualify for residence at the Farm, a girl could have no dependents living with her and had to be employed by an agency that was deemed to be "essential" to the war effort. She could not have a Civil Service classification above CAF-4 or earn more than $2,100 a year. Rent for a room ranged from $16.50 to $24.50 a month, depending on whether the room was on the ground floor or the second floor.

The individual rooms were attractively furnished, and each hall had large and sufficient bath facilities. Everything one could need, expect or want to make life pleasant and convenient was available within the gates of Arlington Farms. A Recreation

Center seating 1,200 people offered sports events, dances, movies, church services, concerts and theatrical productions. There were laundry facilities and kitchenettes in each hall. As if that wasn't enough, each hall also had craft rooms, music rooms, large reception halls for entertaining visitors, a beauty shop, a library, and a shop that sold everything from hot dogs to prescription medicines. There were also picnic grounds and a bowling alley. Almost *utopian* by today's standards, Arlington Farms, designed for gracious and convenient living, was a City of Girls.

Arlington Farms stood through 1946. Some time after the war, its function fulfilled, it was razed. No doubt there are more than a few elderly ladies throughout our vast land, alumnae of the Farm, who remember the good life in that extraordinary complex. Some never returned to their home states, but stayed in the Washington area to work even after Arlington Farms became a thing of the past. But they all remember "when"!

The Factory

THE FACTORY IN QUESTION CERTAINLY WASN'T THE MOST glamorous of establishments, that's for sure, but it made its existance in the area known for a number of years, and those of us who are "of a certain age" remember it well. It was located somewhere in a vast expanse of land between the railroad tracks that ran alongside of Route 1 and the Potomac River, north of Potomac Yards freight train complex. This was not the sort of place that my mother would take me or my sister to visit for historical or educational purposes.

You could not help but know it was there, because it exuded unpleasant odorous fumes that drifted over the neighborhood on a regular basis—depending on which way the wind was blowing! Owned by the Norton family, the fertilizer factory thrived in that bucolic setting for quite a while, long before anyone worried about environmental issues and air pollution.

When things were working up to speed at the plant, and the odors were unmistakable, I used to hear my mother mention that they must have gotten a new shipment of dead horses over at the fertilizer factory.

What do they do with dead horses nowadays? Thank goodness, they don't bring them over to a fertilizer factory right in our back yard!

Still There

THE HOUSE NEXT DOOR TO ME HAS BEEN THERE FOR AS LONG AS I can remember. I have been told that Mr. Moore had it built in 1925 and it remained the Moore's house until a few years after Mrs. Moore's death in the '50s. There were three children in the family and the youngest girl (the sole surviving Moore) was one of my childhood playmates. We still see each other when she comes back east from Missouri for her annual visit.

A very important part of the house was a big green wooden swing that was suspended from the porch ceiling by heavy metal chains. That swing would hold three or four little kids, and it was usually kept busy all summer long giving us great rides to and fro. Mrs Moore was a very busy, magnificent seamstress. She would sit and swing very gently in that swing on nice summer days to do the delicate hand work on whatever her current project happened to be—from wedding dresses to dancing costumes to little girls' dresses.

The house was rental property for a couple of years, and then the Moore adult children decided to sell it. The new owners lived there for a long time and had four beautiful children before they decided to move down to a lovely mountain-top home in the Shenandoah Valley. But the house with the green swing was not put on the market, and my family still enjoys a warm friendship with our former next-door neighbors.

Through all the many tenants and even through a horribly devastating fire several years ago, that old green wooden swing has survived. It is still there hanging from the ceiling on those heavy chains for the pleasure of whoever happens to be living there at any given time, or waiting for some little kids to come back and pump some new life into it. For me it brings back great memories of days gone by.

The Hub

EVEN BEFORE MY PARENTS MOVED HERE IN 1923, THERE WAS A fire house at the corner of Frazier and Jefferson Avenues (now 23rd and S. Eads). By the time the '20s were slipping away, that fire house was too small and too antiquated to take care of the growing community. It was a thrill to watch a beautiful new red brick fire house rising at that site in about 1927. In those early days, firefighting duties were performed by resident volunteers. Our dedicated volunteer fire chief, Glenn Bixler, lived in the 600 block of Frazier Avenue, so he had the pleasure of having the fire siren on the top of his house. When he got word of a fire, he turned on that siren, and it could be heard all over the neighborhood. Then our brave volunteers would scurry to the station from all directions.

As time went on, the community outgrew the volunteer operation's capability, and county-paid firemen were assigned to man the station. A rescue squad was also added somewhere along the line. "Buddy" LeRoy, Fire Chief at the station from 1940–1960—a valuable early "import" from D.C., and his wife, Elizabeth, a life-long resident—only very recently moved from their long-time Virginia Highlands home to a nearby retirement community.

Volunteer or county operated, our red brick fire house was really the hub of the neighborhood because it had a very nice meeting room on the second floor. Neighborhood dances, parties, movies, plays, dancing lessons for the young folks, musical programs, civic meetings, and so forth—all were held in that hall. The Ladies Auxillary of the Fire Department, the Ladies Aid Society of the Methodist Church, and others often held Saturday bake sales there. Those bake sales were always enthusiastic gatherings, and my mother and I spent a lot of time making lemon meringue pies, baked beans, and potato salad for those occasions. Other local ladies were known for their own specialties, and all of us would receive individual requests for certain items ahead of time.

The neighborhood just kept growing and growing, but there was no space on that corner to enlarge the fire house. So a new and larger one was built on S. Hayes Street, as it curves around from 15th into 18th Street. The new fire house opened its doors for business in mid-December 1977. That whole government complex—which includes the Library and Community Center—is sitting right smack on what used to be a portion of our infamous sprawling clay pits.

And now, an additional special high-tech fire house is being built next to 1977 building. These two stations will be working together as a team to continue taking care of our community.

The Dump

IT CERTAINLY WASN'T THE PRETTIEST THING IN THE WORLD, that's for sure, but there it was—for quite a few years—as Aurora Hills and Virginia Highlands were developed and populated. That local dump smoldered along—24/7—for more years than anyone wants to remember.

The smoky eyesore was located on the land between Four Mile Run and the southern side of S. Glebe Road, spreading out a bit east and west from where S. Eads Street now dead ends. Anything that you couldn't use in your compost heap, or bury in your own backyard or burn in your little black kitchen "trash burner" went down to the dump. There were a lot of things you could deal with at home—leaves, tree trimmings, yard clippings, newspapers, *Ladies Home Journals, True Confessions,* old love letters and sundry household trash. Anti-burning laws hadn't even been thought about in those days.

How things got to the dump in the very early days was a mystery to a little girl. My guess is that you just had to get them there the best way you could. But the dump remained with us for a quite few years after the county garbage and trash system began making regularly scheduled pick-ups. The demise of the dump came some time after the construction of the incinerator at S. Glebe Road and S. Eads Street, which then developed into our full-blown incinerator/sewage treatment/hazardous waste complex.

Such as is the character of dumps all over the world. Our local dump was also a great place for all of God's living creatures (including humans) to scavenge—something like a hazardous "finders-keepers" yard sale.

The incinerator/sewage treatment facility sprawling along S. Eads Street may have its problems. Still, we can be thankful that the dump got dumped. Good riddance!

The Spice of Life

IT WAS A VARIETY STORE. ACTUALLY IT WAS MORE THAN THAT. It was a *great* variety store. It always amazed me that there could be so much assorted merchandise in such a small building. Maybe the walls were made of rubber! In any event, even if you didn't see what you wanted, more often than not one of the Hymans could find it for you in the storage area of Hyman's Store.

Mr. and Mrs. Hyman lived in a cute little house on the north side of 23rd Street, directly across from Our Lady of Lourdes church. The house is still there, although there have been a couple of alterations and additions down through the years. Their little variety store was—where else?—in the 500 block of 23rd Street from the mid-'40s until the mid-to-late-'60s.

Hyman's was an extraordinary place. It had everything—well not exactly *everything,* but *just about* everything that you needed right now. So, if you broke your last sewing machine needle in the middle of a project, you were in luck, because Hyman's would save the day. You could find all sorts of necessities for the baby and young kids, work clothes hats and boots for men, rain gear for all, men's and women's undergarments, nightgowns, lounging slippers, sewing, knitting, and embroidery notions, brightly colored ribbons, and much, much more.

One time I needed a gold-colored zipper for a dancing costume for my daughter. I went to D.C., Alexandria, and Arlandria—to no avail. Well—I could have saved myself a lot of time and bother if I had gone to Hyman's in the first place, because there it was, just waiting for me to find it. I should have figured that out early on!

We lost our little variety store in the midst of the great 23rd Street shuffle as Crystal City was developed in the '60s and, sadly, nothing has ever come along since to fill the gap.

The Clay Pits and Beyond

IN THE EARLY '20S AND '30S, WHEN OUR COMMUNITY WAS VERY young, the Washington Terracotta Company had a thriving brick-making operation on a large tract of land stretching north of 18th Street roughly between what are now South Fern and South Hayes Streets. Everyone called the area the Clay Pits. Although it wasn't good for growing tomatoes, that red Virginia clay sure made great bricks!

It was a semi-forbidden place to go, but, I have to confess, the neighborhood kids (including me) loved to go there and play among the big rounded brick ovens and flat-topped sheds. We climbed up on the sheds and jumped off over and over. We ran rings around all those ovens, and broke the daily monotony of the workers with our antics. It was fun to watch the men working those ovens. They never seemed to mind that we were under foot. If anyone asked, it was easy to explain why we were there: It was on the way to Arlington Junction, where other school friends lived.

By the late '50s and early '60s, when my children were old enough to notice the change, the brick yards had been moved to the other side of Route 1 and the Washington Terracotta Company decided to do something profitable with all that prime land—clay pits and all. Before long the commercial/residential building boom was moving right along, and various kinds of buildings were going up all around.

So those humble Virginia red clay pits and the surrounding open fields have been transformed gradually, and sometimes painfully, over the years into what you see today—our very modern and, for the most part, sophisticated and attractive residential and shopping metropolis.

But before the Crystal Towers complex was built, from around 1961–67, there was something else of note on that property.[14]

14 See "Gone But Not Forgotten."

School Bells

THAT INTERESTING LOOKING RED BRICK QUEEN ANNE-STYLE building up on Arlington Ridge Road is the old Hume School, which was built in the early 1890s. A two-room elementary school for the children from the surrounding farms and near-by suburbs, Hume School had classes from the first through the eighth grades. There was an auditorium with a stage on the second floor and a flight of steps from the school yard down the steep hill to help the students from the eastern down-side make it to the top of that hill. Although the school was closed in 1956, those steps are still there and much of the exterior of the building still looks like it did in 1893. In 1963 the building was renovated and reopened as the Arlington Historical Museum. It remains a wonderful symbol of our neighborhood's fascinating beginnings.

I don't know why my mother didn't send my older sister to Hume School. Instead she went to the Mt. Vernon School in Del Ray. That was perfectly legal, because our part of the world in those days was a part of Alexandria County.[15] We were so glad when Nellie Custis School was built, in 1928, at 23rd and S. Grant Streets[16], so I didn't have to go to Mt. Vernon via the trolley

---

15 Our address in those days was 111 Greene Avenue, Alexandria, Va.

16 After Oakridge Elementary was built and up and running, the county closed Nellie Custis School and sold the building. Over the years the owner—The Sheltered Occupational Center—has remodeled and enlarged the building drastically and conducts a thriving business staffed by adults who are in some way physically challenged but none-the-less well-qualified to perform the tasks at hand This enterprise has made itself an integral part of our neighborhood and has proven to be a real asset in numerous ways.

car, or walk all the way to Hume School and up those steps, to learn my ABCs.

When I went to Nellie Custis School, the front door opened onto a small foyer with wide steps straight ahead leading up to the classrooms and office on the main floor. On each side of the staircase was a down staircase—boys' basement to the left; girls' basement to the right. The basements served as our gym, recess play area, and haven from the storms.

And so, my memory tidbits come from the four-room Nellie Custis School that I attended for six years. Several additions and expansions followed in short order, and by the time my three oldest children were enrolled in Nellie Custis (in the mid-1950s) it had 10 class rooms, up-dated and enlarged rest room facilities, an auditorium and a library, and Gunston Jr. High was on the horizon.

There had been an earlier junior high school, just west of I-95, off of S. Glebe Road and tucked in along side a motel that faced S. Glebe. That was Dolley Madison Jr. High School, and my daughter went there for a year before Gunston was opened. A tunnel from the school under that busy I-95 allowed the students from our side of the highway to come and go in safety. The Dolley Madison Towers apartments now occupy that bit of land.

Random Memories of Nellie Custis School

- Teachers: Miss Kidwell, Miss Warner, Miss Griffith and Miss Glasscock (Principal and 6th grade teacher).
- Fun playing on the hot-air register in the hall at the top of the steps.
- Fear of the strange toilet facilities in the girls' basement,

which had a door only on the teachers' stall. The "facilities" flushed simultaneously according to some mysterious method and schedule, making me fear that someone (most likely me) could at any time be sucked into the system and out into the Potomac River, never to be seen again.

- Miss Griffith tapping us kids on the head with that long, wooden rubber tipped pointer that she seemed to have in her hand most of the time.

- Miss Glasscock's beautiful black evening dress with an uneven hemline—short in front and long in the back— just like today's fashion.

- Distress for not being strong enough to climb to the top of the swing support poles hand-over-hand like all the boys could.

- Being punished by Miss Kidwell for unthinkingly hopping off of the seesaw, causing my playmate who was up in the air to come crashing down to earth with a thud.

- Fun we had making, giving and receiving all those fussy, frilly Valentines each February 14th.

- Pride in having my mother serve as PTA president, and starting a library in the hall of the school, and planting beautiful purple iris from the street to the school steps on both sides of the walk.

- Happiness when it was my turn to ring the bell for recess.

- The beautiful seasonal pictures the teachers created with colored chalk on a special section of the blackboard.

- Not being at all happy to leave my friends and go into the big city for junior high school, which is what my parents for some reason decided I would do.

To Market, To Market

SEVERAL GROCERY STORES HAD SPRUNG UP IN THE NEIGHBOR-
hood by the late '20s and into the '30s and '40s. Each came and
went in its own time—a Sanitary (Safeway's predecessor) in the
500 block of 23rd Street, a Safeway at the corner of 23rd and
Route 1, a DGS (later called Brill's Market) at 23rd and S. Hayes,
the Potomac Market at 23rd and S. Grant, and the Hyland Market
on 20th Street. There also was, at one time, a Grand Union where
we now have the 7–11 at 23rd and S. Eads. But the stand out was
the Jefferson Market, located in the 500 block of 23rd Street,
most likely in the present Cafe Italia building.

The Shapiros and the Metros, two related families who lived
in the neighborhood (the Shapiros on 24th Street, the Metros on
S. Eads Street) owned and operated the Jefferson Market. Mr.
Golden, a neighbor who lived on 24th Street, was the butcher.

The Jefferson Market had everything you would expect in any
grocery store, but it also had various items that you would find
only in speciality high-end stores. Mr. Golden would cut your
meat to order; you could call and place an order (large or small),
charge it or not, and ask to have it delivered. The delivery man
was a good-natured, courteous and reliable young man called Friday. I doubt that Friday was his real name, but it was his name at
the store and to everyone in the community. The Metros and Shapiros knew their customers by name, knew where they lived,
knew how many and what kind of kids they had or did not have,
and made it their business to see that you got what you came to

get and that you liked what you got. Once upon a time, Mr. Golden even weighed my little Chihuahua dog, Chili, on his scales—no charge of course!

By the mid-to-late-'60s, the Jefferson Market was feeling the effects of competition from the new discount supermarkets. In addition, and probably more importantly, the Metros and Shapiros were getting up in age and facing various physical problems. They just wanted to get away from it all and retire while they could still enjoy it. So they phased out their business, sold the building and their homes, and disappeared from the neighborhood.

But all of us old-timers will always have pleasant memories of the Metros, the Shapiros, Mr. Golden, and Friday.

Drive Right In

THEY WERE ALL THE RAGE FROM THE MID TO LATE '30S RIGHT
through the late '70s. Several were scattered across the whole
Northern Virginia area, but our favorite, of course, was our very
own Airport Drive-In Theater. Now what could be more fun than
piling two too many young folks into the car that you borrowed
from your Dad and having a private party, with various movie
idols of the moment as the featured entertainment? Unless, that
is, you would rather just take your best gal there and steal a little
kiss now and then when no one was looking.

The Airport Drive-In Theater dominated a vast tract of
wooded land on the east side of our infamous Route 1, approxi-
mately between what are now 15th and 18th Streets.[17] Its neighbors were few and far between—a brick yard, a wrecking company, a lumber yard, a warehouse or two, and probably several
others just as well forgotten. The theater was the biggest and
brightest structure from the 14th Street bridge to Potomac Yards.
Since it was so close to the Big City, "our" drive-in was also a
mecca for lots of fun-loving "foreigners" from just across the Potomac, where so much open space was scarce.

With a big neon-sign airplane flying across its huge front
(which, in fact, was the back of the movie screen), you knew in no

17 15th Street, before Crystal City was ever thought of, was a one-and-a-half-lane road from
Route 1 to the George Washington Parkway. Its only saving grace was that it was an
adventurous short-cut—going under the railway trestle—to the Washington National
Airport (now the Reagan National Airport).

uncertain terms that you had "arrived"! My oldest son tells me that, in the theater's latter days, it really bothered him that most of the time the propeller on the sign was either flickering or out altogether. No matter, Airport Drive-In had a bustling, well-stocked snack bar and a state-of-the-art "adjust to suit yourself" sound system. Sh-h-h-h—there's a party going on!

The concept and arrival of today's multi-screen theaters signaled the beginning of the end for drive-in theaters throughout the area. However, if changing technology hadn't closed our drive-in, the galloping development of Crystal City, with its concrete and glass corridor, would have. Either way, the Airport Drive-In is now just another charming memory, flickering propeller and all.

It's a Bet

WHEN THE "FOUNDING FATHERS" DEVELOPED AURORA HILLS and Virginia Highlands, the streets and avenues were, in fact, just plain old two-lane dirt roads with fancy names. There were no curbs, but there were sidewalks in some of the more prominent places.

The late Joe Martin, one of the early settlers in the area, loved to tell the story of the day that he and my father were standing at the corner of 23rd and S. Eads (then Frazier and Jefferson Avenues) contemplating the condition of Frazier Avenue following a night of heavy rain. It was a muddy mess, with numerous puddles threatening any courageous traverser.

Eyeing the situation my father, who was a small man with the strength of a little bull, said, "Joe, I bet you a dollar I can walk across Frazier Avenue without getting my feet wet." Joe, being a successful businessman, figured that was a pretty good deal, so he took my father on. "With that," Joe would say, "that little rascal got down on his hands, pulled his body straight up into the air and walked across Frazier Avenue on his hands!"

Joe always got a good laugh out of that and thought the show was well worth his dollar.

At Last—
A Post Office

AURORA HILLS AND VIRGINIA HIGHLANDS WERE GROWING BY leaps and bounds in the '30s, but its stalwart pioneers still had to travel to Alexandria, Clarendon, or Washington, D.C., to even buy a stamp, much less mail a package! Realizing the dire need for postal services in the neighborhood, Mr. Irvin Siegal and Mr. Sam Chernikoff, proprietors of the Jefferson Cleaners and Dyers and good citizens that they were, initiated the necessary arrangements to have a branch office put in place and offered their space and services.

Our much needed postal station opened on July 1, 1936. It was a branch of the Arlington central office and was located in the Jefferson Cleaners at 507 23rd Street, S. The hours were from 8:00 a.m. to 6:00 p.m. You could purchase money orders, register letters, mail packages, secure stamps, envelopes, and post cards and, in fact, transact practically all postal-related business.

And so we were finally on the map, so to speak, and mailing a letter was no longer a nagging chore. The *Community News* announced the opening of our branch Post Office and reminded everyone that letters mailed from there to Alexandria would require three cents postage, while those going to other parts of the county would require only two cents postage.

That Post Office branch later moved to larger quarters on S. Eads Street (in one of the buildings behind the 7-11) before moving, again, to a newly constructed building at 18th and S. Eads. If you've been to our Post Office lately—and who hasn't—you probably have decided that it is time for another move to an even bigger building with appreciably more parking space.

The Trolley Tavern

IT WAS A REPLICA OF AN OLD-FASHIONED TROLLEY CAR. THERE it sat, in all its quaint glory, facing Route 1 on the north side of 23rd Street. Of course, I remember its being there, but I can't recall when it came to the neighborhood, or when it left. My copy of the *Community News* for July 3, 1936, carries an impressive advertisement touting their Virginia Ham and Southern Fried Chicken, as well as home-made ice cream, and the fact that they had kept up with the times and could serve you a nice cold beer. Curb service was also available.

It was around the time when the diner closed that the first Safeway grocery store moved into the newly erected building at that location.

Personally, I think a little Trolley Tavern on that corner would be much more interesting than an underground tunnel to Crystal City. But, for now, we have the tunnel!

Tea Anyone?

IT MIGHT HAVE BEEN ORIGINALLY A VERY CHARMING SUMMER get-away home for a prosperous Washington, D.C., resident because that is what many of the original houses on Arlington Ridge Road were. A couple of them have managed to survive the ravages of time and encroaching development—for now.

In any event, from 1920 to 1963 that lovely white house with all the windows and the quaint well house was Allison's Little Tea House. It was situated on that pronounced peninsula of land, high up on the ridge, wedged between Arlington Ridge Road and S. Lynn Street. Fortunately, when the Little Tea House was razed in 1963 to make way for the Ridge House apartment building, the historic well house was spared. You can see it—a wonderful remnant of by-gone days—from the roadway at the narrow end of that peninsula. It now serves as a pool house for the condos, but the original exterior has not been changed.

Allison's Little Tea House was the kind of place where the Ladies' Club would meet for luncheon or where you would take an out-of-town relative for tea on a balmy June afternoon. It had an aura of genteel elegance about it, without being pretentious. We would often drive by when I was a child, and I longed to stop and have lunch, but those were lean times and we just couldn't do it.

From its high vantage point, Allison's Little Tea House offered a panoramic view of our neighborhood, as well as the Washington, D.C., skyline and the Potomac River wending its way down toward Alexandria. On hot summer days cool breezes danced in and out of the open windows.

Allison's Little Tea House was a delightful little restaurant in a beautiful setting—now just a charming memory.

On the Road

THERE WAS NOTHING LIKE TRAVELLING IN A MODEL T FORD from Aurora Hills, Virginia, to Summerville, South Carolina (just outside of Charleston) in the mid-'20s. I wouldn't have missed it for the world, but I wouldn't want to repeat it either!

My mother did most of the work of packing our clothes and assembling all the gear that we required to ensure our survival en route. My father had the car to worry about—before, during and after the expedition. It wasn't quite like the Conestoga wagons rolling across America but it was a second cousin, at least.

First of all, Daddy had to secure all the luggage and gear to the running boards of the Model T with detachable metal holders. We left the house at about 4:00 a.m. for our two-day excursion. There were no freeways or beltways, and not even too many hard-top roads. Daddy called those bumpy, two-lane dirt roads "washboard roads," and that pretty much tells the story.

Gas stations were few and far between, so every time we happened upon one we would stop and fill up to be sure we would have enough gas and water (Model T's liked a lot of water) to get us to the next oasis in the wilderness. If the kids had to go to the bathroom along the way, well, there were always the woods flanking both sides of any road to anywhere. Since there were no rest areas, McDonalds or Wendy's in those days, Mother packed a portable kerosene stove and food so that we could stop and prepare a nice hot meal whenever we wanted, right there in a little clearing in the woods at the side of the road.

Our overnight accommodations consisted of a room in some farm house that sported a "Tourist" sign at its gate. We didn't need an alarm clock because the roosters were sure to be up crowing and parading around the front porch at the crack of dawn.

There were two swamps to get through—the Dismal Swamp in Virginia and the Pee Dee in South Carolina. And don't think there weren't any alligators or other predators out there to make that trek a bit scary!

We were on our way to South Carolina in that wonderful Tin Lizzy when my father decided to teach my mother to drive. There we were, bumping along one of those washboard roads parallel to a main north/south railroad track. Things weren't going too well in the front seat. In the first place, a Model T Ford wasn't the easiest thing to drive and, in the second place, my father wasn't too patient, and in the third place, I was scared. I got down on my knees on the floor, facing the rear with my elbows on the back seat, and began praying out loud. That was just the straw that broke the camel's back, and spelled the end of Driver's Education 101. Mother never got behind the wheel of a car again. I've always felt a bit guilty about that.

Things to Do

Previous page, clockwise from top left

Old Arlington County Library at 23rd and South Eads Streets
(Library Night, page 107)

Betty Moore, Zula Dietrich, and Dorothy Fatheree
playing ball on 25th Street
(No Kids Allowed, page 15)

Zula in costume on George Washington's 200th birthday
(The Minuet, page 125)

Zula's house when her parents bought it in January, 1923

Music in the Air

MY PLAYMATE WHO LIVED NEXT DOOR—JUST ACROSS TWO adjoining driveways—had a beautiful singing voice. I couldn't carry a tune in a bucket, but I had a grand piano that sat right by a big window facing those driveways, and I could play. A George Washington University language professor, who lived on the corner of 25th and Eads, also played the piano, the violin and the flute. So, every once in a while on a nice summer's day we would throw open all the windows and have our very own concert on the 500 block of 25th Street. First, I would start playing a song, then my friend would stick her head out of a window singing all the while, and music filled the air. This was the professor's cue to pick up his violin and join in. It was a lot of fun.

At other times, I would go down to the professor's house and play some classical number on the piano while he joined in on the violin. Once in a while, we would treat the neighbors to a piano duet. Also, sometimes there would be just a solo concert with the singer, and the professor or me at the piano.

It seems that people just don't do things like that any more. Everyone is so busy worrying about crab grass in the yard, or going to Little League games, or getting to the mall before all the parking spaces are gone. Or they just lounge in their air-conditioned houses with the TV on and the rest of the world shut out. Is spontaneous music a program if nobody hears it?

Library Night

BY THE EARLY 1930S, ARLINGTON COUNTY HAD SHOWN SOME interest in the library that my mother had started in the hall of Nellie Custis School a few years previously. The county provided a small room in the building at the corner of So. Eads and 23rd Streets (predecessor of the Burke & Herbert Bank building), and allocated funds for supplies and acquisitions, utilities, and so forth. It was called the Martha Duncan Library. There was no paid staff, however. My mother and one of our neighbors, assisted by my sister and me, checked books in and out and shelved them. Exactly what hours the library was open, I no longer recall. Wednesday night, however, was Library Night, and my mother was always there.

Library Night brought out all the young people who could read and walk or ride bicycles and they came from all over. It was, obviously, a big social time. Even so, those children also learned the excitement of a good story and chose their books with great care and interest.

Within a few years, Arlington County made our growing library an official branch of the county library system, and moved it into the entire building on that corner. A paid professional staff was put in place, and it operated on regular county library hours. There it stayed until it moved once more into a new and larger building in the 1970s. The grown-up library that came from that little library seed in the hall of the school is now located, as everyone knows, at 18th and S. Hayes Streets—still near the Rescue Squad!

My mother would be so pleased.

Once Upon
a Trolley Car

LONG BEFORE THE DAYS OF TRAFFIC GRIDLOCK, EIGHT-LANE beltways with their "inner" and "outer" loops, awesome Interstates with confusing signs and interchanges, ramps and cloverleaf configurations and other life-threatening features, there were trolley cars in our little corner of the world. Those beautiful and fun trolleys clanked along the tracks from Washington, D.C., to Mt. Vernon, passing through Virginia Highlands and Aurora Hills along the way. The tracks were located between S. Eads Street and Route 1, with stops at 18th, 20th, 23rd, and 26th Streets.

A shopping trip to downtown Washington, D.C., or to Alexandria in the '20s was a lot of fun, because it always meant a round-trip on the trolley. And what a ride! The seats were yellowish wicker, and there was a big brass horn attached to the outside of the car. Whenever anything threatened our path, or to announce our arrival at the various stations on the line, the conductor would blast that horn. And sometimes, he may also have done it just for fun, or to amuse the children on board.

Arlington Junction was at the south end of the 14th Street Bridge (about where the "Paperclip Building" is now). It was at this point that the trolley changed from "underground" power to "overhead" power. Extending from the top of the trolley car was a long rigid pole that clipped onto the electric "life line" rigged up above. Then the car really bounced and clanked along at a brisk clip, with sparks flying from the overhead pole as it made its way through a number of other little individually named neighborhoods—DelRay, Hume Springs, Cottage City, Rosemont (to mention a few)—before arriving in downtown Alexandria.

In the late '20s or very early '30s, those wonderful trolley cars were replaced by the latest innovation—red busses. After that, we had to cross Route 1 and stand in the dirt on the shoulder of the road to wait for a bus.[18] From fun to flat in one short lesson!

There is nothing like an old-fashioned trolley car ride to revive your spirits. San Francisco knows all about that, and would never, ever retire its ancient cable car system—I hope!

---

18 Washington, D.C., kept its electric street cars operating for quite a few years after our trolley line disappeared—up into the '50s or '60s—but the cars were newer and more sophisticated and didn't bounce or clang or have a memorable personality of their own.

Let It Snow, Let It Snow

IT IS ALMOST BEYOND BELIEF TODAY, BUT THERE REALLY WAS A time in my life—in the late '20s and throughout the '30s—when a good snowfall would coax the county authorities into closing 23rd Street—just for the fun of sledding! So all the kids would pray for snow, find their warm mittens, sharpen those Flexible Flyers and wait for the CLOSED sign to go up.

There would be a fire in a tall metal can at the top of the hill. That is where we gathered to warm our hands, compare sleds and start off on one of many fast rides down the hill. It was a long walk back, but there was always a lot of company—and youth prevailed.

At one time, there was even a bobsled in operation, made by twin boys who lived in Arlington Junction. In between our solo or double-decker belly-flop rides down the hill, we would line up for turns on that. The bobsled would hold about six people, all squashed together, straddling the long plank seat, with their feet on the running boards and each rider's arms and knees tight around the person in front of him. One of the twins steered in the front while the other handled the back rudder. That sled could really *go*!

There were a lot of spills and thrills and even a couple of unfortunate accidents on the 23rd Street hill before increasing motor traffic forced the county to call a halt to seasonal sled traffic, but it sure was a lark while it lasted.

Dressing Up

AS A CHILD, IN THE SUMMER MONTHS I COULD PLAY FREELY ALL morning. I could make mud villages, dig up my own garden, gather earthworms and tadpoles, clean the chicken house and the rabbit hutch, roller skate, play jacks and get as dirty as any kid could, wallowing around in the great outdoors. However, there was a time in the mid-afternoon when all of that came to a halt and I was required to "dress up for the afternoon." This involved a bath, of course, and a complete change of clothes. No more knickers or "bloomers" allowed. (Look *that* up in *Webster's*.)

This was a hard and fast rule at my house, and every summer afternoon I found myself sitting primly on the front porch learning to be a "lady." All little girls had to learn to embroider useful household things, like doilies, pillowcases, table runners, and so forth. We also had to shell peas and lima beans, snap green beans, and help prepare other foods for the evening meal.

When I was quite young my father bought something new and wonderful called a radio, and so we could listen to "The Lady Next Door," who told great children's stories every afternoon. There was no more painful punishment for misbehavior than to have that program withheld—not even a few swipes of the peach tree switch my mother always kept handy! As my friends and I grew older, we would sometimes play a card game called Pounce (a group game, but similar to Solitaire) and, of course, we always had a couple of good books at hand and an ongoing jigsaw puzzle.

And so that is how it was before the Age of the Computer.

We of that era managed to live through such a bleak existence. We even thought that we were having fun.

Don't Scratch!

WAY BACK IN MEDIEVAL TIMES, WHEN I WAS GROWING UP, HAV-
ing a swimming pool in this area was just stupid wishful thinking. Alexandria had a public pool where the older kids occasion-
ally went. My summer swimming took place at the Municipal
Pools—two free-admission public pools located on the western
side of the Washington Monument grounds in D.C. With the
trolley car line to ride on, getting there was no problem. My problem was convincing my sister and her friends that I would not get
in their way or cause them any grief—or drown on their watch!!

Three days of the week were Girls' Days and three days were
Boys' Days. Maybe the girls went Monday, Wednesday and Friday, or maybe that was for boys. Whichever it was, it never
changed and that was a help. One pool was for lessons and the
other was for splashing around and practicing what you should
have learned in the first pool. I couldn't touch the bottom at
either pool, so I didn't get any lessons and spent my time dog pad-
dling or treading water near the edge of the pool or sitting on the
side with my feet dangling in the water, trying not to get in
anyone's way.

All of us—big girls and tag-along little sisters—had a com-
mon problem the entire summer. We all wanted to go to the pool,
of course, but to get in we had to pass inspection. That involved
getting into a bathing suit, taking a shower and standing in line
while an attendant determined if you were sporting any open
sores, infected mosquito bites, or the like. Mosquito control was

pretty primitive back in those early days, so we could all count on being bitten numerous times from one week to the next. Poison Ivy was another lurking villain. The trick was not to *scratch*. If you scratched and the spot turned red and got a bit angry looking, you wouldn't pass inspection.

We all had some close calls at the pool, but I don't remember ever being denied admittance. However, I do recall the constant anxiety every summer over those never-ending itching mosquito bites.

Sparklers and Fountains

EVERY FOURTH OF JULY ALL THE KIDS ON OUR BLOCK OR VERY close by knew they could come to our backyard fireworks party. My husband always had a big fireworks stand in front of his Minute Grill on Jefferson Davis Highway just south of 23rd Street. And, naturally, we had an ample supply of whatever kind of fireworks were legal in Virginia at the time.

We started our party while it was still daylight, with fried chicken, potato salad and a big jelly roll cake that looked like a huge firecracker. There was an unlimited supply of Cokes, Yahoo, orange and grape soda and 7-Up. We always had several crates of all kinds of sodas in our basement and, even when it wasn't the Fourth of July, the neighborhood children knew they were always welcome to "sneak" in our side door like little thieves and help themselves to a soda.

Just before dark we organized the children into a big semicircle across the yard facing our water-filled inflated plastic wading pool. First we had sparklers; every child got a box of them, and then waited for his turn to have an adult light each sparkler. Wave your sparkler in front of you, OK. Print your name in the air with the sparkler, OK. Run with the sparkler, Go Home! We had little fountains, medium-sized fountains and large fountains, which we lit a safe distance from the children. And there were pinwheels, nailed to a tree, and Roman Candles, held in the hand to shoot into our neighbor's backyard (with permission). And so it went, until everyone had his fill of food and fireworks, and all the debris had been tossed into that water filled pool so that there were no "hot spots" to worry about. If they wanted anything more exciting, the kids still had time to coax their parents into taking them down to the Monument grounds for the *big* display.

I haven't seen anyone setting off any fireworks of any kind for years, but we always had a great time back in those good old days at our simple little backyard fireworks parties.

Che Mugwumps

ANYBODY REMEMBER ARTHUR GODFREY? HE NEVER STOPPED being a real character, on and off radio and TV, in the early days. He was a stocky, freckled-faced, rugged-looking redhead with a wide grin and a decided limp—the result of an unfortunate auto accident. He started as a staff announcer and went on to get his own radio program in 1934 at one of the local stations—WJSV. At that time WJSV was housed in an attractive little red brick building sitting all alone on the west side of the George Washington Parkway, just across the road from where the airport is now. Godfrey had a daily morning show that started at 6:00 a.m.; however, he lived in Leesburg, and off and on he didn't quite make it by 6:00 a.m. Someone always covered for him as he laughed and joked his way, first to local fame and then to not just one but two weekly nationally broadcast live TV shows out of New York City: "Arthur Godfrey's Talent Scouts" (1945–1957) and "Arthur Godfrey and Friends" (1949–1959).

Arthur Godfrey had an impish but charming manner and a natural sense of humor. His talent—aside from playing the ukulele—was being a wonderful, congenial show host. I think he was the first radio host to pan his sponsors. Zlotnick's, a local furrier in downtown Washington, D.C., had a big stuffed polar bear standing out in front of the store. Godfrey used to tell everyone about that big, dirty polar bear on G Street. He also loved to give a local diaper-washing company a hard time. Sales always went up when Godfrey kidded about the products he was hawking.

When I was confined to my bed for six weeks in 1934, Arthur Godfrey awakened everyone in the house every day at 6:00 a.m., thanks to me, a devoted fan. He created the Mugwump Club. It didn't really do anything, but I joined and got a certificate of membership. I cherished that certificate for years . . . until my mother decided to do away with some of the clutter around the house. It was just a fan club, and we card-carrying members were just happy to be called Mugwumps—whatever that meant!

In the mid to late '40s when my husband owned the Leesburg Airport, Arthur Godfrey kept his private plane there. Whenever he and his personal pilot flew down to Florida, he would send or bring back a case of grapefruit or oranges for the airport gang.[19]

That old charming, exceedingly wealthy, scamp was riding high with his success in TV. "Arthur Godfrey & Friends" had a devoted following until one night Mr. Godfrey fired his regular and very popular singer, Julius LaRosa, right on the air and out of the blue. No one—including LaRosa—knew the firing was coming. This did not sit too well with many of Godfrey's viewers, and caused a running feud with two well-known newspaper writers: Dorothy Kilgallen and John Cosby.

Godfrey's last television appearance was in 1973. He was probably still plunking away on that ukulele when he died in 1983 at the age of 80. Arthur Godfrey will long be remembered as the interesting, unpredictable and fun-loving pioneer radio and TV personality who fired Julius LaRosa, but, to me, he will forever be the Mugwump of all Mugwumps!

---

19 Arthur Godfrey later became a licensed pilot.

The Circus Comes to Town

FOR A FEW YEARS IN THE EARLY 1950s, THE MILLS BROTHERS Circus stopped here on the way back to winter headquarters in Florida and put on a show for us suburbanites. The tent and one ring were set up on the east side of Route 1 in the open spaces just a bit south of where the Buchanan House and its adjoining buildings now stand.

This was a small circus, but was both intimate and complete, which made it especially fun for the kids. The seats were rough bleachers set right down on the dirt oval where the elephants lumbered by just to get things started. If you sat on the first row you felt like you should tuck your feet up under the seat before one of those huge elephant feet banged down on your toes. There were trained horses and dogs that did tricks, beautiful ladies riding elephants, acrobats, and the usual "man on the flying trapeze". Thankfully, we didn't have to worry about any lions or tigers being led around the oval! The clowns, of course, stole the show with all of their amusing antics.

My oldest son recalls that for a couple of years—probably in the late '50s or early '60s—when the Mills Brothers dropped in for a visit they set up their shows in the "Clay Pit" area between 18th and 15th Streets and S. Fern Street, roughly where we now have that low, grid-like electrical structure and the Claridge House.

If the Mills Brothers Circus still exists and should come this way again, they would quickly find that there is no space left here for exercising the elephants—much less throwing up a tent and having a show.

It would have to just roll right on by! What a shame!

Moo Cow Moo

THEY LIVED IN A DISTINCTIVE LOOKING SAND-COLORED STUCCO house sitting up on a little knoll on a double lot at the northwest corner of 20th and S. Fern Streets. The Nagels and their two daughters were very early settlers in Virginia Highlands. The house is still there, exactly like it was all those years ago, double lot and all.

Although the Nagels were a part of my earliest memories of the community, I never knew them well. My mother said that Mr. Nagel had a small herd of cows on what was then a sprawling tract of land between the railroad tracks and the river. However, she never took my sister and me to visit the cows. Mr. Nagel quite likely sold the raw milk to one of the local dairies, which then processed and bottled it. We always had a little grey steel insulated box at our back door, and Thompson's Dairy delivered milk to us on a regular schedule and picked up our empty glass bottles for reuse. Plastic and heavy paper containers came much later.

In those days—before homogenized milk became the norm— I remember (with loathing) that the cream, often clotted, rose to the top of the bottle. It took a lot of shaking to get everything back together again, and even at that, it never stayed "together" long enough to suit me. Homogenized milk was a truly great innovation.

Sooner or later, the dairy farm was overcome by development, and the Nagels and their cows moved on. It is amazing to realize how much has changed on that tract of land during my lifetime, and it fills me with wonder and awe. Actually, it would be quite refreshing now to see a few cows grazing over by the river.

The Minuet

ONCE UPON A TIME IT WAS 1932 ALL AROUND THE WORLD. IN the United States of America it was a time for national celebration of the 1732 birth of our first President, George Washington. And so we called it the Bicentennial Year. Everyone got into the act at one place or another, in one fashion or another, throughout the entire year.

My up-the-street playmate and I got *our* little act together at the suggestion of her elocution teacher. Our mothers made us beautiful colorful silk Martha Washington-type dresses that swept the floor, and bought us white cotton wigs just like you see in pictures of the ladies in those days of long-ago.

Someone must have handled our "bookings," because we found ourselves going to all sorts of ladies' church, school, club and civic functions. All decked out in our long dresses and wigs, my friend would recite a little piece about life in Colonial times as I softly played Beethoven's Minuet in G on the piano.

Hollywood never called, but I treasure a large tinted picture of me in that Martha Washington dress and wig, and recall with joy our own cameo role in that 1932 nationwide celebration.

What's News?

WHETHER IT WAS JUST THAT YOU AND YOUR DAUGHTER HAD travelled to Fredericksburg over the past week-end to visit an ailing aunt, or your neighbor had sailed from New York on the *Queen Mary* to spend the summer touring Europe, it made our wonderful, exclusively local *Community News*. Glen Bixler, who worked fulltime for the now defunct *Washington Star* newspaper, was Editor-in-Chief, reporter, page formatter, circulation department, and "chief cook and bottle washer" for our little paper—which was his 1933 brainchild and our joy. Only the actual printing was done off-site.

Fortunately, I possess some examples: a couple of very fragile yellowed and crispy pages of the July 3, 1936, edition which tell of my sister's beautiful wedding at Calvary Methodist Church, and some equally fragile pages from the August 16, 1935, edition letting everyone know that my mother and I journeyed to Summerville, S.C. to visit her family for a week or so. Of course, we also went to Folly Beach in Charleston and got painfully sunburned, but that never made the headlines.

The *Community News* never editorialized about politics, crime, religion, world affairs, disasters, or hunger in India. However, it did let its readers know about up-coming county and community meetings and newsworthy events of interest and concern to the residents of Aurora Hills, Virginia Highlands, Arlington Ridge Road and Oakcrest. The paper was distributed, free-of-charge, on the first and third Fridays of each month.

Each edition featured several amusing cartoons as well as an impressive array of advertisements from our local merchants reminding us of their services and products. And I saw a notice on one page that Ruth Flaherty would be in charge of Fay's Beauty Shop from August 20 to 26 while Fay McCoy was taking a short vacation!

In the mid and late '30s, some of Louise and Margaret Bixler's girl friends used to drop in at the Bixler home on the proper Fridays to help fold the papers for distribution by the husky young volunteers recruited from throughout the various areas of the neighborhood. As small as it was, my paper-folding role at that time was a lot of fun. I always looked forward to joining in.

A bit of our very own identity disappeared when the *Community News* ceased publication in 1951, but there are still a few of us left who will tell you that nothing can ever fill that special little empty spot the *Community News* left behind.

Wheels to Go

MOST OF THE KIDS IN MY NEIGHBORHOOD HAD ROLLER SKATES. Not the kind of skates you see today, however. Our metal skates clipped onto the soles of our shoes and had four small metal ball-bearing wheels and a leather ankle strap. We proudly kept our skates in tip-top shape, cleaning and oiling the wheels to get the best possible performance out of them. A skate key always hung on a string around our necks so that we could secure the grip of the clamps and tighten the wheels when necessary. And we skated all over the neighborhood, too. What else were sidewalks for?

Our favorite roller skating adventure was to skate—laboriously—all the way up Washington Avenue (now 26th Street) to the top of the hill where it joined Frazier Avenue (now 23rd Street). Then the fun began! Off we would go down the hill as fast as we could, jumping the curbs and clumping across the streets as we went. In those days, as I remember, there were some hickory trees along the way, so once in a while we would stop and crack a few nuts open with a large stone and tediously pick out some of the meat. Then it was off down the hill again. The ride ended at the trolley station. Once around the station and then it was back up the hill for another trip down.

When going up that hill wasn't too tempting, we were free to skate anywhere there was a sidewalk—around and around the block or up one side and down another. We got to know all the cracks and bumps and hazards in all the surrounding sidewalks.

We knew where the best blocks were as well as which ones to avoid for whatever reason.

Alas, sidewalk skating as I knew it seems to be a thing of the past but, for me and my friends, it was a "big deal" and a lot of fun in spite of those inevitable falls and skinned up knees.

Depression Years

THE STOCK MARKET CRASH, THE BANK CLOSINGS, AND THE
ensuing Great Depression didn't affect me very much. I was too
young to understand the political and financial problems facing
my world. However, looking back, I realize that the Depression
spanned most of my childhood and teenage years. The country
was just recovering somewhat when I graduated from high school.
Even after I finished business college, things were still a bit
tight.[20]

Fortunately, although my father had to take a ten percent salary cut at one time, he never lost his job at the Treasury Department. We always had a warm home, food on the table and clothes
to wear. My mother worked very hard all those years, running her
household while maintaining a big vegetable garden, raising her
chickens, and making most of her two daughters' clothes. We
usually had one or two room-and-boarders in those days who
shared our home and table, thus supplementing my father's salary
nicely. I just thought that was the way things were supposed to
be—nobody had money to splurge. For me, a five-cent bottle of
Nehi grape was a special treat.

In retrospect, there are things I remember about the depression days which at the time I just took for granted: the panhan-
dlers on F Street in downtown D.C.; the men selling pencils and

---

20 My first regular full-time job was as a GS-4 stenographer with the U.S. government, and
the salary was $1,440.00 per year.

apples on the street corners; a procession of homeless men who came to our side door asking for food; the little girl who cried when her only dress got torn as she was playing in our yard; the beautiful young lady across the street who searched for cigarette butts on the ground and saved the tobacco until she had enough to roll herself a cigarette, and the bonus marchers' camp in Washington, which I had to pass every day coming home from school.

No one was turned away from our side door. Mother always fixed those men a simple meal with coffee or a cold drink and served it to them on a china plate. They would sit on our back steps in the shade of my father's big grape arbor and eat their meals and soothe their souls. As for that torn dress, mother mended it right away, and by the next day had started making the child another little cotton dress.

Certainly no one would welcome another depression, but isn't it a pity that in our present materialistic world, it takes so much to excite the younger generation? A new sweater or blouse to wear to school or that yard of beautiful green wool that an aunt gave me long, long ago to make a skirt was enough to delight my adolescent heart.

A Little Girl's Christmas

SOMEWHERE, SOMEHOW, BETWEEN THEN AND NOW, CHRIST-
mas has changed. Everyone, sooner or later, realizes that a little,
fat, jolly man, dressed in a red suit, can't possibly fly around the
world in one night in a sleigh with eight tiny reindeer—even if
reindeer could really fly—going up and down chimneys all along
the way, and leaving presents under every child's brightly lit
Christmas tree. Slowly but surely—almost without our object-
ing—Christmas has become a whiz-bang merchandizing extrava-
ganza.

But I remember when . . .

Mother started making her heavy, dark fruit cakes just after
Thanksgiving. Then came the dozens and dozens and dozens of
cookies. There were plain sugar ones cut into Santas or reindeer or
stars or trees, with red and green sugar on top. There were fancier
cookies, too: little gingerbread boys with red candy buttons
marching down their tummies and black raisin eyes, chocolate
and vanilla pinwheels, diamond-shaped crisps with a pecan in the
center, butterscotch slices that melted in your mouth, and others.
After these goodies came out of the oven and cooled, they were
carefully put in huge tin lard cans and hidden away in the dark
corners of our attic. My sister and I, of course, knew they were
there, but we were on our honor never to open a single lid. Once
in a while we might go up to the attic to make sure those trea-

sured tins were still waiting for us, but we never dared to peek inside.

Christmas Eve was always set aside for trimming the tree and decorating the house. Magically, the cookies would suddenly appear that evening as we slaved away polishing the floors with that big, old, miserable, lead-weighted brush. When that was done, we hung hand-made red and green crepe paper chains from the corners into the center of each downstairs room. Then right in the middle, where the chains met, we placed big, red paper Christmas bells that we had furled open and fastened with a tiny metal clip.

My father never had much of a Christmas during his childhood. He was one of ten children in a hard-working family. In addition, his Pennsylvania Dutch mother was a Dunkard—the so-called plain people—and didn't make too much of Christmas. Daddy liked to pretend that Christmas was unimportant, but we knew that deep down he really enjoyed being a part of it. Every year he proudly brought home a beautifully shaped live Christmas tree, constructed a stand for it, and patiently struggled putting on all the bright red, blue, yellow and green lights. That done, he would retire to his favorite chair to ponder over his next move in one of his on-going play-by-mail checkers games. The best part was up to the girls, and we made sure that our tree was always beautiful, with bright glass ornaments and silvery strands of icicles dripping from the branches. It just had to be the prettiest one in the whole neighborhood! Of all the ornaments, my favorite was a golden glass airplane with Santa Claus waving greetings to all from the cockpit. Year after year it was my special treat to hang the flying Santa on the tree.

Finally, weary, and full of cookies and milk and high hopes, we hung our limp, empty stockings on the mantle and trundled off to bed. Without fail, on Christmas morning our stockings would be fat and bulging with oranges, apples, candy canes, old-fashioned hard Christmas candy, and all kinds of nuts.

Nothing ever changed our Christmas morning routine. It was set in stone like the Ten Commandments by my mother, and never questioned by my sister or me. There would be no peeking at our presents—and no breakfast—before we went to the sunrise candlelight service at Calvary Methodist Church on 23rd Street. After church came breakfast. After breakfast, came the presents. Amen!

Every Christmas morning before dawn, I would carry out my self-appointed duty and tiptoe downstairs to the piano to play "Silent Night" as loud as possible. This got everyone in the house stirring—probably the neighbors, too. Excited, we hurriedly bundled up in our Sunday best and happily set off on foot for church. Christmas was here at last!

It was always dark and cold, but I have such warm memories of walking the several blocks to the church, listening all along the way to a stalwart small brass band playing Christmas carols on the church steps. Perhaps the musicians, with their half-frozen fingers and lips, hit a few off-key notes. The music they made was still heavenly—a hallowed, peaceful Christmas moment—never to be forgotten.

Have you ever heard a brass band playing Christmas carols on the steps of a church at the crack of dawn? Can you imagine it? I have, and I can, and I am so glad!